101 CLEVER
CARD
TRICKS

101 CLEVER CARD TRICKS

Cara Frost-Sharratt

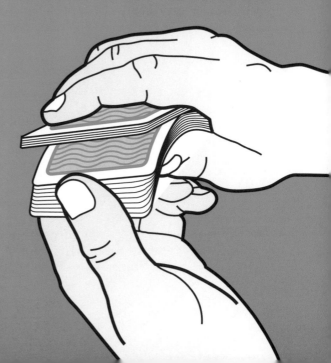

hamlyn

An Hachette UK Company
www.hachette.co.uk

First published in Great Britain in 2006 by Hamlyn,
a division of Octopus Publishing Group Ltd
Carmelite House, 50 Victoria Embankment, London EC4Y 0DZ
www.octopusbooksusa.com

First published in North America in 2013
This edition published in 2016

Distributed in the US by Hachette Book Group
1290 Avenue of the Americas, 4th and 5th Floors, New York, NY 10104

Distributed in Canada by Canadian Manda Group
664 Annette St., Toronto, Ontario, Canada M6S 2C8

ISBN 978-0-600-63418-8

Card designs based on Waddingtons No. 1 Playing Cards.

WADDINGTONS NO. 1 PLAYING CARDS © 2005 Winning Moves UK Ltd.
Used with kind permission of Winning Moves.

Printed and bound in China
10 9 8 7

Publisher's note
The text has been written from the point-of-view of a right-handed
magician. For shuffling the pack, reverse the instructions given for left-
handed magicians to read 'left' for 'right' and vice versa.

Contents

Introduction

If you have ever been to a party where a magician has moved from one table to the next entertaining guests with card tricks then you will be familiar with the buzz and thrill that magic can create. People love to be entertained and there is nothing to beat a card trick that leaves an audience amazed and confused. A good trick can have people pondering and guessing for days and, as the old saying goes, a good magician never reveals his secrets.

In this book you will discover a wide range of tricks that will help build up both your repertoire and reputation. Do not worry if you are new to card tricks: step-by-step explanations and accompanying diagrams make it easy for you to learn in no time at all and you will soon be dazzling family and friends with your skills. All the tricks in this book can be mastered easily by the novice magician, although some will require a little practice before you perform them in front of an audience.

From very simple tricks for absolute beginners to those that rely on mathematical principles and others that require props or a little preparation, this book should prove an invaluable reference for every budding magician. Each trick has a skill-level rating that ranges from one to five. This will make it easier for you to choose the tricks you want to try. Those with a skill level of one or two are perfect for beginners, as they require few special skills and can be mastered in minutes. Those with higher skill levels either require mastery of a number of sleights, or take longer to prepare and perform, often with more complicated steps to remember.

Back to basics

In addition to being adept at regular shuffling for a slick performance, there are a number of false shuffles and basic sleights that are needed for many of the tricks in the book. A good number of tricks require you to keep a card, or group of cards, either at the top or bottom of the pack, while others cannot be performed without a 'double lift' or 'palming' a card. If the technology is new to you, this section will explain all you need to know to get you started, and will take you through all the essential moves.

Shuffling

Although there are a number of ways to shuffle cards, the move known as the 'overhand' shuffle is the best one to use when performing card tricks, because it is the easiest one to adapt for false shuffling.

The overhand shuffle

The following description is for right-handed people. If you are left-handed, simply carry out the same steps using the opposite hands.

1 Start with the pack face down in your left hand, with all four fingers below the pack and your thumb resting on top.

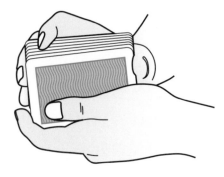

2 Using your right hand, grasp the majority of the pack with your fingers holding the top (short) edge of the cards and your thumb holding the bottom edge (above).

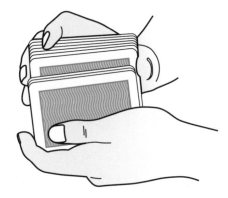

3 Raise the cards in your right hand up and over those that remain in your left hand, and use the thumb of the left hand to drag down a number of cards – say ten or so – at a time (above).

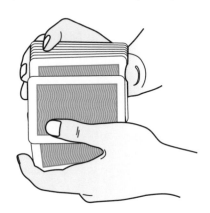

4 These dragged-down cards should fall on top of those in your left hand, ready for the next lot to follow (above).

5 Repeat the steps until all the cards are shuffled and begin again, working through the pack two to three times before starting the trick.

False shuffles

False shuffles are essential skills to learn, as they are used in so many card tricks. If you practise long enough your audience will never guess what you are doing and, in fact, a false shuffle can really add to the authenticity of a card trick in which you are trying to convince the audience that you couldn't possibly have positioned a card in a certain place.

Top of the heap

1 To keep a card in place at the top of the pack, hold the pack in your left hand, face down, with your thumb on top of the pack and your fingers holding it around the back.

2 Grasp the pack from underneath with your right hand so, positioning the fingers of your right hand on the top edge of the pack and your right thumb on the bottom edge. Now lift up the majority of the cards with your right hand and as you bring them over the top of the remaining cards in your left hand, subtly slide your top card towards you a little with your left thumb. This is now referred to as an 'injogged' card (above).

3 Now lower the main pack and use your left thumb to pull down a small pile of the cards from your right hand. Continue doing this until all the cards are used. Try not to make the pile too squared up otherwise the injogged card will become obvious to the audience.

4 When all the cards have been shuffled, use your right thumb to make a break above the injogged card and move this, and the pile of playing cards behind it, over the top of the pack and drop them down on the others (above). Your chosen card is now back on the top.

Down under

1 To keep a card in place at the bottom of the pack, perform the shuffle as above, but as you grasp the majority of cards in your right hand, use the fingers of your left hand to grip the bottom card and drag it down behind the pile in your left hand (right).

2 The bottom card remains in place and you can continue dropping small piles of cards over the top, safe in the knowledge that the card will remain where it is.

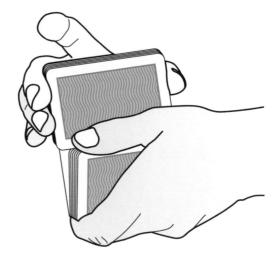

Shuffle up

1 To move a card from the bottom of the pack to the top, simply perform a normal shuffle – that is, grasp the majority of cards in your right hand and let them drop on top of the cards in your left hand.

2 As you approach the end of the pack you need to make sure that the last pile you drop contains just one card – the bottom card. Let it drop on to the rest so that it now becomes the card at the top of the pack (right).

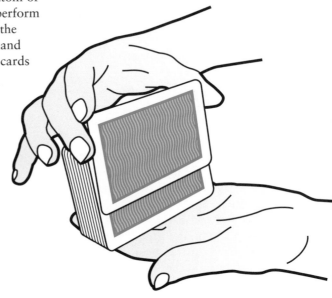

Top to bottom

1 To move a card from the top of
the pack to the bottom begin the
shuffle as for Top of the Heap (see
page 9). In grasping the majority of
the pack with your right hand, make
sure you take all but the top card.

2 Perform the rest of the shuffle as
normal, knowing that the top card
is now at the bottom of the pack.

Fanning out cards

Several tricks in this book involve
you fanning out an entire pack
of cards so that a member of the
audience can pick a card. This can be
quite difficult to achieve, especially
for people with small hands. For
these tricks, it is best to keep the fan
tight if possible. Square up the cards
to start and then, holding them in
your left hand, use your right hand
to spreads the cards in a circular
motion, fanning them so that the top
card moves towards the right and the
bottom card is fanned out to the left,
until you have a fan you can hold

easily with your thumbs to the front
of it and your fingers to the rear.
Keeping the fan tight is particularly
good advice, as a number of the
tricks require you to keep the cards
at the bottom out of sight, or use
marked cards, which would be
revealed if the fan was too loose.
Alternatives to fanning out the whole
pack are spreading the cards out face
down on a table or flat surface, or
offering just a section of the pack for
the volunteer to choose from as you
shuffle through the pack of cards in
your hands.

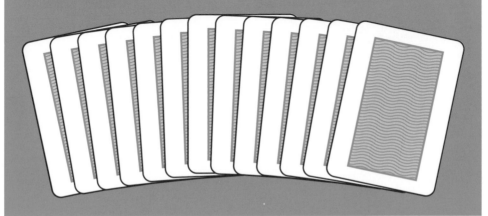

All stay together

Certain tricks require you to keep a number of cards in a particular order at the bottom or the top of the pack.

1 To keep a group of cards at the base of the pack, perform a basic shuffle, making sure that the last batch contains all the cards required plus a few extra.

2 When you let these drop into the palm of your left hand, keep a break between them and the rest of the pack using your left thumb (above).

3 Now you can begin a second shuffle, using just the cards behind the break. Once the shuffle is complete, the batch that was originally at the bottom of pack will be there once more.

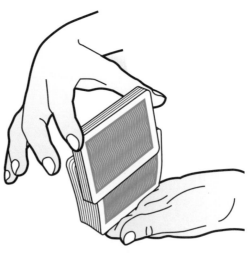

4 To keep a section of cards at the top of the pack, simply reverse the process: ensure that the first pile you drop into your left hand contains the cards you require plus a few extra. When pulling down the next and subsequent batches, maintain a break with the first section with the tip of your left index finger. Once all the cards have been dropped, just take the cards behind the break and bring them to the front of the pack (above).

The double lift

This is an easy move and is used to great effect in a number of card tricks. It involves lifting two cards from the top of the pack at once in order to fool the audience into thinking that you are showing them just the top card. The idea is that you want to keep the identity of the real top card a secret for the time being. You can then slide off or remove the real top card as and when necessary for the completion of the trick.

1 You need to hold the pack – or pile of cards you are using – firmly in your left hand, face down and preferably with your fingers and thumb grasping the long edges, leaving as little of the pack visible to the audience as possible. The top few cards should be held loosely so that they are easy to manoeuvre.

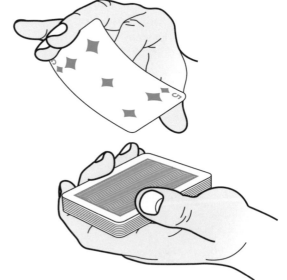

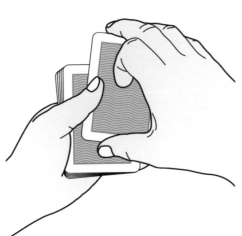

2 Bring your right hand over the top of the pack to grip it top and bottom with the middle two fingers of your hand and your thumb (above).

3 Grip the top card of the pack and move your fingers very slightly to get a grip on the second card as well. Making sure that the cards are aligned exactly, so the audience cannot tell there are two of them, lift them and turn them to a vertical position immediately to show the audience (above). Replace the cards on the pack and perform the trick as required.

Palming a card

This is another indispensable skill that will allow you to perform a greater number of card tricks. It requires some practice before incorporating it into your routine but is definitely worth the effort.

1 Hold the face-down pack of cards in your left hand and twist it at an angle towards you.

2 Perform the same movement as you would if going to square up the deck – indeed, this is what you want your audience to think you are doing. So, bring your right hand over the top of the pack and allow it to rest lightly on top of the cards, with the right side of your hand pressing down a little more firmly.

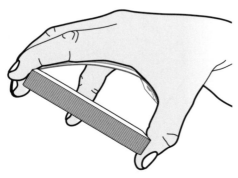

3 Use your left thumb to separate the top card from the rest of the pack and grip this with the little finger and right side of your right hand. Use your left thumb to push the card more firmly into your right palm and allow your hand to bend naturally, the card following the shape (above).

4 You can now move your right hand away, in as natural a movement as possible, while keeping the audience focused on the main pack. Talk to the crowd and maintain eye contact while you carry out the manoeuvre.

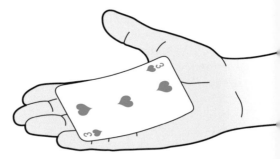

5 You can either put the palmed card in your pocket or keep it in your right hand depending on the trick requirements (above).

6 If you need to replace the palmed card, again pretend to be squaring up the pack and bring your right hand back over the top of the deck. Then simply release the card and square it up.

Simply amazing

The tricks in this section require the minimum level of skill when it comes to performing them. They are all very easy to master with a little practice and, despite their simplicity, are extremely effective when it comes to duping the audience. Most of these acts involve nothing more than basic trickery, such as preparing the deck in advance or glimpsing a card during a shuffle. Others introduce useful techniques like the false shuffle or double lift, which are necessary for progressing to the more complex tricks in a magician's repertoire. Newcomers to the art will find this the perfect place to begin.

Cut and locate

A member of the audience chooses a card from the pack. She memorizes the card and returns it to the top of the pack before cutting it. The magician then flips through the pack until he finds the chosen card. This is a good trick to perfect if you are a beginner, as it requires a peek at the pack but no special skills.

Skill level ♦

How to do it

1 Shuffle the pack in front of your audience. While doing so, have a quick look at the card at the bottom of the pack.

2 Ask for a volunteer. Fan out the pack (see page 11) and ask the spectator to choose any card, memorize it and replace it on top of the pack.

3 Place the deck on the table and ask the spectator to cut the cards and complete the cut by placing the bottom pile on top (below).

Top tip

By talking to your audience during the shuffle you will distract them from the pack of cards for long enough to take a quick look at the bottom card.

4 Square up the pack and slowly start dealing the cards on to the table, turning them face up as you go. When you reach the card that was the bottom card you peeked at, you know that the next one will be the spectator's chosen card. Hover over it to keep the audience in suspense, and then flip it over and reveal to all.

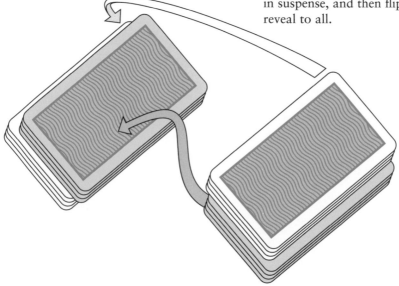

The shuffle deduction

A spectator memorizes one of ten cards offered and its position in the pack. Following a swift process of elimination, the magician is left with a single card – the chosen card. This is a great trick that can be performed anywhere to any number of people. It is quick and easy so it makes a great interval between longer tricks that need more preparation.

Skill level ♦

How to do it

1 Shuffle the pack and deal the top ten cards face down on to the table. Set aside the remaining cards. Ask for a volunteer from your audience.

2 Fan out the ten cards (see page 11) and ask the volunteer to choose one of them, memorize it and then return it to the fan. Tell her to remember the position of the card in the fan by counting the cards from her left (below).

3 Square up the cards, remove the top five cards keeping them in the same order and place them underneath the bottom five. Ask the spectator to tell you the position of her card and now count off that number of cards from the top of the pile and place them on the bottom of the pile. So, for example, if her card was the third one in, you count off three cards.

4 Square up the pile once more and eliminate the cards in the following manner: take the top card and move it to the bottom of the pile then take the next card and place it on the table. Repeat this process (one underneath, one on the table) until you're left holding one card. Turn it face up and the spectator will see that it is the card she chose.

4th card in

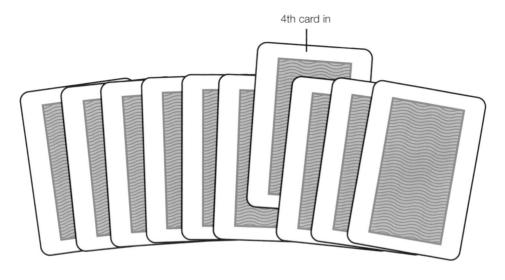

Process of elimination

A spectator chooses and memorizes a card from ten offered by the magician. After moving cards to the bottom of the pile and eliminating others, the spectator ends up with one card face down in his hand. He turns it over to discover it is the card he picked. This trick works on the same principle as The Shuffle Deduction (see page 17) but this time the spectator is locating his own card.

Skill level ◆◆

How to do it

1 Shuffle the pack and ask for a volunteer. See if he wants to shuffle the cards as well and then take them back and deal the top ten cards face up in a fan on to the table in front of him (see page 11).

2 Ask the spectator to look at the cards and memorize one of them. He also needs to remember the position of the card in the fan. Tell him to remember the position of the card in the fan by counting the cards from his right.

3 Ask the spectator to square up the pile. Take the cards from him and, holding the pile face down in your hand, move three cards from the bottom of the pile to the top, one by one.

4 Now ask the spectator to reveal what position his chosen card was in the original fan. He then needs to transfer that number of cards, one by one, from the bottom of the pile to the top.

5 Now ask the spectator to place the top card on the table and place the next card on the bottom of the pile. He must continue doing this until he is left holding just one card. Ask him to turn the card over and it will be his.

Foolproof card guess

A spectator cuts a shuffled pack and memorizes the top card on his pile. The magician is able to guess his card. This is a very quick trick that uses the card glimpse.

Skill level ♦

How to do it

1 Shuffle the pack in front of your audience. As you do so, glimpse the bottom card and use a false shuffle to bring that card to the top of the pack (see page 10).

2 Square up the pack and place it on the table. Ask a volunteer to cut the pack wherever he likes.

3 Now you have to be both quick and careful. You need to give the spectator the top pile, as this contains the card you memorized, but you must make it look as though he is getting the bottom half of the randomly cut pack.

4 Ask him to look at the top card of his pile. Appear to concentrate hard then reveal the identity of the card.

Top tip

To ensure that the audience does not notice that you are giving the spectator the wrong half of the cut pack of cards, keep talking in order to distract attention away from the cards.

An orderly fashion

The cards in a pack are flipped over repeatedly in batches until they are well and truly mixed – some face up, the rest face down. With just one cut and three taps the cards are all miraculously face up once more. This is an effective trick that is quick and easy to perform. It will fool everyone once – but probably no more than that.

Skill level ◆

How to do it

1 Shuffle the pack well in front of your audience and very roughly fan out the cards in your hands (see page 11). Separate a small pile of cards from the main pack, flip them over and return them to the top of the pack (above).

Top tip

Always try to keep the pile of cards that is about to be turned over squared up in your hand so that the audience cannot see that they are not mixed randomly.

2 Take the same section of cards, plus a few more from underneath, and turn the whole pile over, again returning it to the top of the pack (above).

3 Repeat the process along the fan, working quickly and roughly to keep your audience in a state of confusion. By the time you reach the end of the pack it will look as if all the cards are completely mixed up when, in actual fact, all you have done is neatly split the pack so that one half is face up and the other face down.

4 Tell your audience that you are now going to split the pack, distracting them no longer than it takes for you to locate the spot where the piles separate. Cut the cards, placing one pile face down on the table and flipping the other pile over on top so that all the cards are now face down.

5 Tap the top of the pack three times with your knuckles and slowly fan out the cards to reveal that they have 'miraculously' been returned to their original order – all facing the same way.

Leader of the pack

The magician shuffles the pack in front of the audience and reveals the top card before returning it to the middle of the pack. The magician taps the pack on the table three times and turns over the top card to show that the revealed card has returned to its original position. This is one of those really simple tricks that will nevertheless leave your audience confused and impressed! It only takes a minute to perform so it is ideal for use in the middle of a routine, between two longer tricks.

Skill level ♦♦

How to do it

1 Shuffle the pack in front of your audience. Next, instead of turning over the top card to show the audience, use a double lift so that the card you actually reveal is the second one down (see page 13).

2 Slide the real top card away from the pack and, keeping it face down so the audience cannot see it, insert the card somewhere in the centre of the pack.

3 Wear a look of concentration as you tap the pack three times on the table. Slowly peel off the top card – the same one you showed the audience at the beginning of the trick.

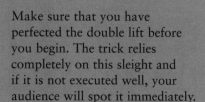

Top tip

Make sure that you have perfected the double lift before you begin. The trick relies completely on this sleight and if it is not executed well, your audience will spot it immediately.

Facing up to the facts

Any five red and five black cards are removed from the pack. Half are reversed then the whole stack is shuffled well and placed behind the magician's back. When the stack is split and returned to the table in front of the audience, the same number of cards is face up in each pile and they are all the same colour, too.

Skill level ♦

How to do it

1 Remove any five red and any five black cards from the pack and set aside the remaining cards.

2 Place the five black cards face down on top of the face-up red cards (below) and shuffle the whole stack well in front of the audience.

3 Hold the cards behind your back and split them into two stacks of five. Turn one set over then set both stacks down on the table. Spread out the two piles and there will be the same number of face-up cards in each pile – those in one pile being red and those in the other pile being black (below).

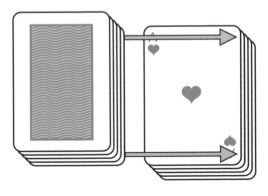

Top tip

This trick will not work if any of the cards get flipped over during the shuffle, so do not shuffle the cards too vigorously.

Out of the box

A spectator chooses a card from the pack. The magician puts the pack back in its box and the spectator inserts her card in the middle. The magician shakes the box, pulls out the cards and the spectator's card is the only one that is face up in the pack.

Skill level ♦♦

You will need
A card box.

Preparation
Reverse the bottom card of the pack before starting the performance.

How to do it

1 Perform a false shuffle so that the bottom card stays in place (see page 10) and ensure that the audience does not see that the card is face up.

2 Fan out the cards (see page 11), again concealing the bottom card, and ask a spectator to pick any card from the pack.

3 Square up the pack, subtly turning it over as you do, so that all the cards are now face up, apart from the top card, which is face down. Put the cards in the box and ask the spectator to insert her card anywhere in the pack. She will assume that her face-down card is going into a face-down pack (above).

Top tip

Make sure you talk to the audience whenever you turn the pack over. This will distract attention away from what you are doing.

4 Close the box and shake the pack, telling the audience that you are going to try to make the spectator's card turn over. As you are shaking the box, turn it over so that the cards are now all face down again, apart from the bottom card and the spectator's card.

5 Remove the cards from the pack and fan them out, concealing the bottom card (below). The spectator's card will be the only face-up card in the pack!

Empty your pockets

A member of the audience picks a card, looks at it and returns it to the pack, which is then shuffled well. The magician waves his hands over the pack, clicks his fingers or performs any other show-stopping turn while telling the waiting audience that the chosen card will be the only one facing up when the pack is fanned out. There will be murmurs of disappointment as this turns out to be a false claim but the magician redeems himself to gasps of astonishment as he pulls the spectator's card from his pocket!

Skill level ♦♦

You will need
Any identical card from another pack.

Preparation
Before you start, place one of the identical cards in your pocket and make sure the other is at the top of the pack.

How to do it
1 In front of your audience, divide the pack into four stacks, remembering which stack contains the all-important rogue card.

2 Ask a willing spectator to choose two out of the four stacks of cards. If the stacks she chooses contain the one with the trick card, hold on to them and discard the others. If not, put both the chosen stacks to one side and retain the stacks with the trick card (right).

Top tips

• Practise this trick a few times so that you can instinctively discard or retain the correct stacks – you need to do this quickly to keep your audience from working out how the trick works.

• Try to look genuinely surprised when your spectator's chosen card is not face up at the end. This will make the final stage of the trick even more effective!

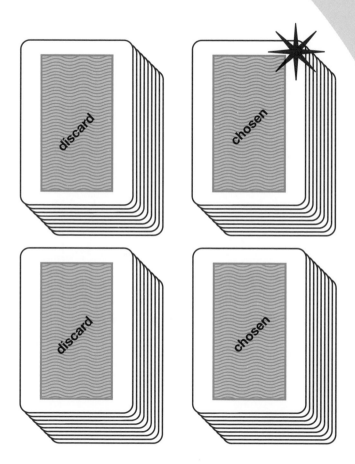

3 Ask the spectator to choose one stack and, again, if it is the one containing the trick card, hold on to it – if not, discard it. Either way, you should end up with the stack containing the trick card.

4 Give the top card (the trick card) to your spectator to look at, then reassemble the whole pack and ask the spectator to replace the card on top. Shuffle the pack well and tell the audience that the card will end up reversed in the pack. Of course, when you fan out the deck it is not reversed, so you pull it from your pocket instead.

The thieving Joker

A spectator picks a card and places it face up on top of the pack. The pack is then cut and the magician tells the audience that the spectator's card will be the only face-up card in the pack. However, when the magician fans through the pack, it is a Joker that is face up. Meanwhile, the spectator's card has completely disappeared.

Skill level ♦♦

You will need
A Joker. Double-sided sticky tape.

Preparation
This trick can be performed in a number of ways and it is a good opener to a set. There is a little preparation beforehand but the trick itself is simple. Before you begin the trick, take the Joker and place a tiny piece of double-sided sticky tape on the back of the card. Now place the Joker face up at the bottom of the face-down pack.

Top tip

It is obviously very important that the audience doesn't see the face-up Joker at the beginning of the trick so, when you are fanning out the cards, be sure to keep the bottom few cards together.

How to do it

1 Fan out the cards in front of your audience (see page 11), being careful to conceal the Joker at the bottom of the pack. Ask a spectator to choose and remove any card, then square up the pack and tell him to replace his card face up on top of the pack (below).

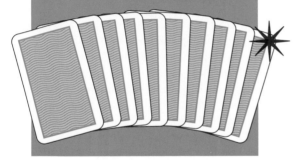

2 Keeping the pack of cards in your hand so that the Joker doesn't stick to the table, cut the pack, putting the cut section down on the table and placing the other pile on top (right).

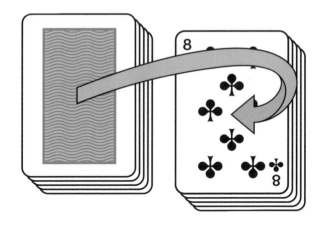

3 Square up the pack – you want the Joker and the spectator's card to be completely flush. While squaring up the cards, press your thumb down on top and your fingers underneath to make sure the two cards stick together.

4 Now fan out the cards and tell your audience that the spectator's card will be the only face-up card. Instead of the spectator's card, however, they will see the upturned Joker (above). Look a little confused and fan through again just to make sure.

5 Remove the Joker from the pack and place it on the table, slightly away from the audience. Now turn the rest of the pack face up and hand it to the spectator, telling him to go through and find his card. Of course, he won't be able to and he will think that his card has simply vanished from the pack.

Simply amazing

Top deck

A spectator shuffles the pack, cuts it, and changes the positions of two cards, as instructed by the magician. The magician is then able to identify the top three cards on the pile.

Skill level ♦♦

How to do it

1 Hand the pack to a spectator and ask him to shuffle.

2 When the pack is returned to you, say you have forgotten to remove the Joker and quickly fan through the pack (see page 11), removing any card that you like. Set it aside, face down. It does not matter which card you remove, this is simply an excuse to view the pack. What you need to do is memorize the values of the three cards that come after the first card in the fan (these will be to your left as you face the fan (above right)). Make sure that you also memorize the positions of these cards.

3 Now you can perform a false shuffle, being careful not to disturb the top four cards, as these need to remain in the same place (see page 12).

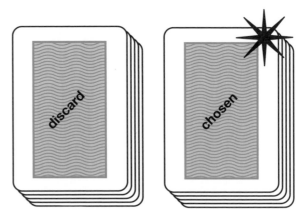

4 Square up the pack and place it on the table. Ask the spectator to make a cut and place the two piles side by side. Ask him to select one pile and, if he chooses the pile with your cards in, remove the other pile; if not, remove the pile he selected (above).

5 You are now left with the pile containing the memorized cards. Ask the spectator to remove the top card and place it in the middle of the pile. Next ask him to remove the next three cards from the top of the pile and place them face down on the table.

  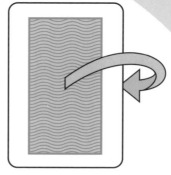

6 It is now time for you to reveal the values of the three memorized cards. Ask the spectator to turn the cards over one at a time to prove your predictions are correct (above).

Top tip

When you are starting out, it is probably best to perform this trick by simply revealing the values of the cards. When you have had enough practice and think you can remember the suits as well try it – it will make the trick even more impressive.

A choice of twelve

Twelve cards are laid out face up on the table. With his back to the audience, the magician gives a set of instructions to a spectator and is then able to tell the audience which card the spectator has finished on. This is a really easy trick to master and another good one to start off with, as you can use it to build confidence at the beginning of a show.

Skill level ◆

How to do it

1 Remove any six red and any six black cards from the pack and set the remaining cards aside.

2 Lay the 12 cards face up on the table in front of your audience, following the diagram opposite. So, row one will be black, red, black; row two will be black, red, red; row three will be red, red, black; and row four red, black, black (right).

3 Ask for a volunteer from the audience and turn your back so you cannot see the cards. Give your spectator the following instructions:

• To choose any black card and place her finger on it.

• To move either up or down to the red card that is the closest to the card she has chosen.

• To move her finger to the right or left now, to locate the closest black card.

• To move her finger diagonally to locate the closest red card.

• To move her finger either up or down to locate the closest black card.

4 Reveal to your audience that the playing card that the spectator has landed on is the black card in the centre of the bottom row and turn back to face your audience and to enjoy their amazement and applause!

Top tips

• No matter which black card the spectator chooses to start with, the instructions are given in such a way that her finger will always end on the black card in the centre of the bottom row.

• This trick is best performed to the same audience only once, as it is a simple self-working trick that won't keep them amazed on repeat performances. It is a great one to practise on people while you are learning the ropes, however, and you should be able to build up to more complicated tricks quickly once you have mastered it.

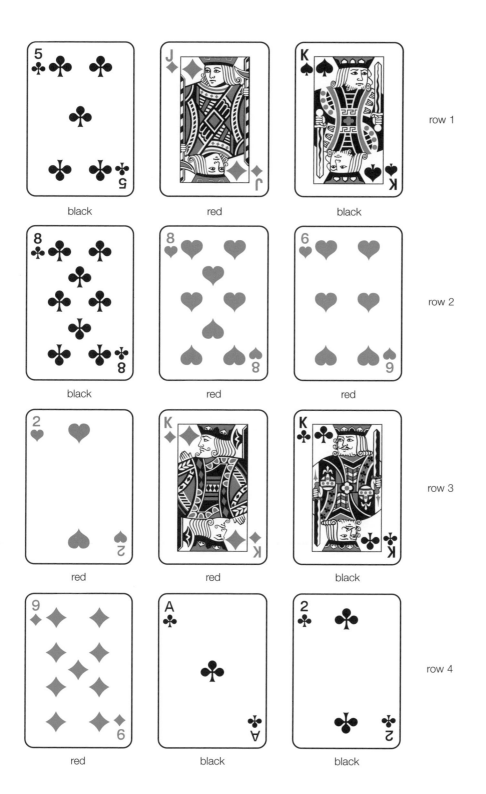

black   red   black   row 1

black   red   red   row 2

red   red   black   row 3

red   black   black   row 4

Simply amazing   **33**

Counting down

A spectator chooses a card from the pack. The card is replaced and the magician begins counting off cards from the bottom of the pack, stopping at the spectator's card.

Skill level ♦

How to do it

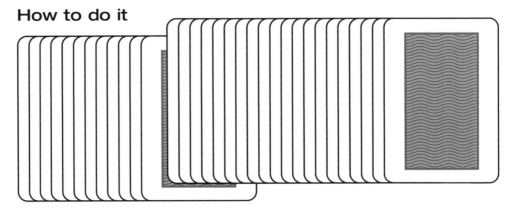

1 Shuffle the cards in front of your audience. Fan the cards out (see page 11) and, as you do, discretely count twelve cards from the bottom of the pack. Push the rest of the pack up and away from this group slightly, so it is easy to separate them (above).

2 Ask a spectator to choose a card and memorize it. While he is doing this, loosely gather together the two piles (the main pack and the twelve cards) and open them as if you've just randomly cut the pack here. Indicate for the spectator to replace his card in the cut and square up the pack.

3 Now you simply have to slide off twelve cards from the bottom of the pack, face down on to the table. When you reach the thirteenth card, turn it face up and it will be the card that was chosen by the spectator.

Variation

This trick can also be performed using a marker card. Before beginning the trick, make a tiny bend in the top left corner of any card. While you are fanning out the pack for the spectator, locate this card and make your cut just after it. Get the spectator to replace his card and then you can deal from the top of the pack, knowing that when you reach the marker card, the spectator's card will be the one that follows.

The suit won't shuffle

A complete suit is removed from the pack and the magician asks a member of the audience to give instructions to deal the cards. No matter how many times he does this, the suit still remains in consecutive order.

Skill level ♦

How to do it

1 Remove all the cards of any suit from the pack and arrange them in their correct order, from Ace through to King. Place them spread out on the table to show the audience (below).

2 Invite a member of the audience to help with the trick. Gather the pile and turn it over so the cards are face down then ask the spectator to give specific instructions for you to deal the pile of cards.

3 He must tell you either to 'single deal' or 'twist deal' each card until all the cards have been dealt. Single deal means simply placing the first card on the table. A twist deal is where you remove the first card, place it underneath the following card in the pile and then place them both on to the dealt pile.

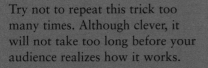

Top tip

Try not to repeat this trick too many times. Although clever, it will not take too long before your audience realizes how it works.

4 Once all the cards have been dealt, pick them up and turn them face up to reveal the suit in the correct order! You can go through the pile twice before revealing the cards if you like and they will still remain in the correct order at the end.

Magnetic cards

A spectator cuts a pack of cards, gives half to the magician and keeps the other half. They both choose a card from their respective piles and memorize it before the pack is put back together. When the pack is fanned out, the two chosen cards appear next to each other.

Skill level ♦

This trick involves glimpsing the bottom card and you need to be confident that you can do so with just the tiniest glance in order to be convincing.

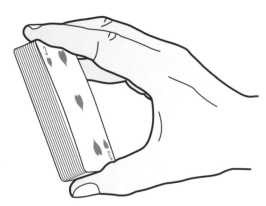

How to do it

1 Ask a member of the audience to cut the pack. She chooses whichever half she wants and gives you the other half.

2 You must each shuffle your own pile of cards and, while you are doing this, you glimpse and memorize the card at the bottom of your pile (above).

Top tip

Find your own method for glimpsing cards without being detected, as it is a useful skill that appears in a number of card tricks. This is a good trick for practice as it is easy to take a glimpse of the bottom card while the spectator is busy shuffling her own pile of cards.

3 Ask the spectator to choose any card from her pile, memorize it and place it face down on top of the pile. Tell her that you are doing the same. In actual fact, you do not need to do this, as the only card you need to remember is the one at the bottom of the pile. Just move any card to the top of your pile, pretending to memorize it.

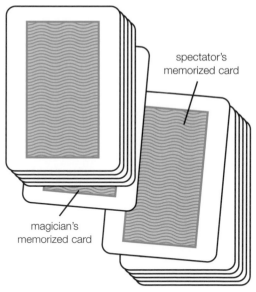

spectator's memorized card

magician's memorized card

4 Both put your piles of cards face down and squared up on the table then place your pile on top of the spectator's. Square them up once more (above).

5 Now you can tell the audience what your chosen card was – the one you memorized at the bottom of your pile, which will now be next to the spectator's chosen card in the pack.

6 Holding one short edge of the pack firmly, riffle – or flick – through the cards at the opposite edge, telling the audience that you are going to try to bring the two cards together using special magnetic forces. Hand the pack to the spectator and ask her to fan the cards out (see page 11) and locate her card – yours will be right next to it.

Role reversal

A spectator chooses and memorizes a card before returning it to the pack. The magician shuffles the pack and tells the audience that the spectator's card will return to the top. When it doesn't, the magician tries the bottom of the pack but the card is not there either. Looking confused the magician fans out the pack and the spectator's card is the only face-down card in the middle of the pack. This trick employs all the basic skills that you need to have mastered before moving on to more complicated tricks. It uses the double lift, the false shuffle and turning a card, yet the trick itself is easy and effective.

Skill level ◆◆

How to do it

1 Shuffle the pack of cards in front of your audience and ask for a volunteer. Fan out the cards (see page 11) and ask the volunteer to pick one and memorize it. Square up the pack and ask him to replace the card on top.

2 Perform a false shuffle so that the spectator's card stays on top of the pack then square up the pack again (see page 9).

3 Tell your audience that you have made the spectator's card return to the top of the pack. Perform a double lift (see page 13), revealing the second card down and look surprised when the volunteer tells you that this is not his card. Keep the card(s) face up and place them back on the pack.

4 Tell the audience that you suspect the spectator's card might have gone to the bottom of the pack by mistake and turn the pack over to show the bottom card. Obviously this will not be his card either and now you must look doubly confused.

5 Keep your audience occupied by talking to them, as you need to distract their attention for the next part of the trick. With the pack still face up, you now need to turn the bottom card over. This will leave just the spectator's card facing a different direction (right).

6 Cut the deck, being careful not to let the audience spot the face-down card. Tell them you're going to fan through the cards so that the spectator can pick out his card and you will try the trick again.

7 When you fan the cards out, there will be one face-down card. Tell the spectator to turn it over and he will see that it is his (below).

Colour code

The magician fans out a pack of cards face down in front of the audience and asks a spectator to choose a card, memorize it and return it to the pack. The magician then cuts the pack, squares it up and flips it over. He fans through once more to reveal that there is now one face-down card in the pack and it is a different colour. The magician turns it over to reveal that this is the spectator's card.

Skill level ♦

You will need
Any identical card from a pack of another colour.

Preparation
Select one card from a pack of a different colour – say red, when your main pack is blue. Place the red card, face up, second from bottom in the main pack. Now place the blue equivalent of this card face down at the top of the pack.

How to do it
1 In front of your audience, cut about one-third of the pack, flip the cards over and place them back on top of the pack. Now cut about half the pack and, again, flip the cards over and place them back on the pack.

2 Ask for a volunteer. Fan out the pack (the first cards should be face up) until you reach the first face-down card and ask the spectator to remove and memorize it. Discard the face-up cards and ask the spectator to replace her card back on the pack.

3 Cut the pack of cards, putting the top half underneath. Square up the pack and flip it over so that the cards are now face up. Fan out the cards (see page 11). There will be one face-down card among the others, which will be a different colour to the main pack. Flip it over to reveal that it is the spectator's card (below).

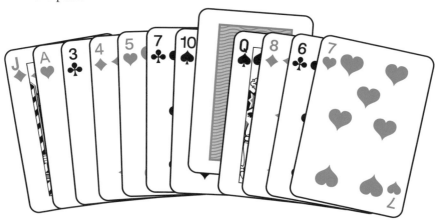

Sleight of hand

A good number of card tricks rely on the magician making manoeuvres that go undetected by the audience and, in most cases, success lies in practising the moves over and over again. This section presents a handful of classic tricks that you can use to improve your dexterity and lightness of touch. All of the basic sleights of hand are included – from flipping cards and performing false shuffles to palming a card and using double lifts. Once confident enough to face an audience, you will be able to perform with such flair that you will leave spectators in awe of your skill as they try to figure tricks out for themselves.

Staying power

A spectator chooses any two cards from a fanned out pack. He then returns the cards to the middle and the magician shuffles the pack. With a flick of the hand the pack falls away, leaving just two cards in the magician's hand – the ones chosen by the spectator. This trick will really show off your sleight skills. When performed well, it looks amazing.

Skill level ♦♦♦

How to do it

1 Shuffle the pack well in front of your audience and ask for a volunteer. Fan out the cards in front of him (see page 11) and ask him to choose and remove any two cards from the pack. Tell him to show the cards to the audience but to keep them out of your view.

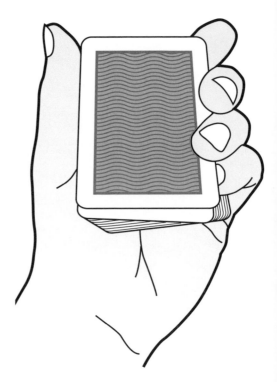

2 Square up the pack and cut it in half, placing the top half on the table. Ask the spectator to place his two cards on the pile in your hand. As he does so, make a break between the two cards while, at the same time, putting the other half of the pack back on top (above). Keep the break so that you now have one of the cards at the top of the bottom pile and the other at the bottom of the top pile.

3 You now need to get these two cards to the top and bottom of the pack. The easiest way to do this is to pretend to square up the pack and make a new cut. Then you can perform a false shuffle to convince the audience that the cards are truly lost in the pack, but making sure the top and bottom cards stay in place (see pages 9–10).

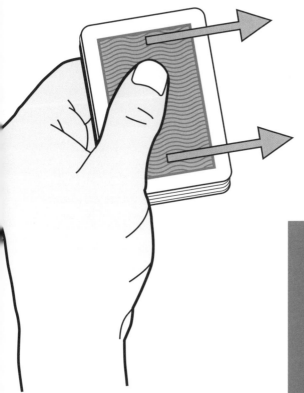

4 Hold the pack of cards in your left hand with your fingers on the bottom and your thumb pushing down on top of the pack. Motion that you are going to flick the whole pack on to the table (left). The cards will fall away, leaving just the top and bottom cards. Turn these over and place them on the table, revealing that they are the cards chosen by the spectator.

Top tip

You need to put reasonable pressure on the cards before you flick the pack in order to make sure that the top and bottom cards stay in your hand. Do not worry about the rest of the cards flying out all over the place – this will just add to the drama!

The flipping trick

A spectator picks a card, memorizes it and returns it to the pack without showing it to anyone. With a flick of the wrist, the card miraculously reveals itself face up in a fan of cards that are all face down. This is a variation of Out of the Box (see page 24) and is another trick that appears to flip a card over in the pack.

Skill level ◆◆

Preparation
Before starting the trick, place the pack face up in front of you. Turn the top card over so that it is face down and turn the whole pack over so that the card is now on the bottom (below).

How to do it

1 Ask for a volunteer. Fan the cards out face down in front of the spectator (see page 11), being careful not to reveal the card facing up at the bottom of the pack. Ask her to remove a card and memorize it.

2 As you square up the cards, flip the pack over so that the odd card is now face down and the cards below are all face up. Split the pack, opening it just enough for a card to be inserted, moving the top half of the split slightly forwards as you do so to ensure the upturned cards are hidden, and ask your spectator to replace her card face down within the pack so you cannot see it.

3 Put the pack behind your back, flip over the top card so that it now faces the same way as all the others and bring the pack back out in front of you.

4 Slowly fan the cards out in front of your spectator and her card will be revealed as the only face-up card in the entire pack.

Top tip

Once you become more adept at this trick, you can try flipping the top card over without putting your hands behind your back. This will make the trick even more amazing.

Slip and slide

The magician slides cards from a face-down deck until a member of the audience says 'Stop'. The magician then tells the audience the identity of the card that the spectator stopped at. On turning the card over, it is revealed to be correct!

Skill level ◆◆

How to do it

1 Shuffle the pack well in front of your audience, glimpsing the bottom card as you do so.

2 Square up the pack and place it flat and face down in one hand. With your other hand, you need to put your thumb under the pack and your fingers on top, so that your hand is reaching lengthways along the pack.

3 Ask for a volunteer from the audience and tell her to say 'Stop' whenever she likes as you slowly slide cards back towards you from the top of the pack with your fingers, one at a time. Tell your audience that you will be able to predict the card that you are asked to stop at.

4 As you slide the cards towards you from the top of the pack you must also slide the bottom card of the pack towards you with your thumb. Then, when the spectator tells you to stop, you slide the bottom card fully out to meet the rest of the pile, pulling them away together. Your memorized card will be at the bottom of the pile (right).

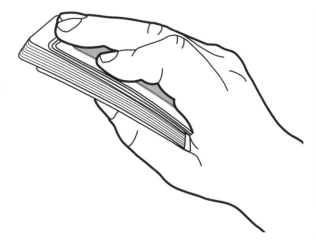

Top tip

By explaining that you are going to predict the card as you perform this trick, you should distract the audience from the fact that you are moving the bottom card as well as those on top.

5 You are aware of the identity of this card so now you can tell your audience your prediction. Square up the pile and flip it over to reveal that you have guessed correctly.

Hands off

A spectator selects a card, which is then placed in his hand by the magician. The magician selects a second, random, card and makes the two cards exchange places. The spectator is left holding the magician's card.

Skill level ◆◆◆◆

You will need
Any identical card from another pack.

Preparation
Place the two identical cards at the top of the pack before beginning the trick.

How to do it

1 Ask for a volunteer to pick a card from anywhere in the pack, show it to the rest of the audience and memorize it. While he is doing this, as you pretend to square up the pack, hold the cards in your left hand and palm the top card in your right hand (below). This will be one of the two identical cards.

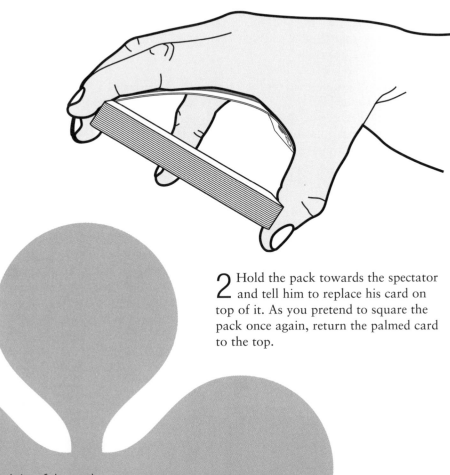

2 Hold the pack towards the spectator and tell him to replace his card on top of it. As you pretend to square the pack once again, return the palmed card to the top.

3 Ask the spectator to place his right hand flat on the table. Perform a double lift (below) to show the audience the spectator's card to confirm that this was the card he chose. Return both cards to the top of the pack and now take just the top card – which will be one of the identical cards – and put this under the spectator's hand. He will believe this to be his chosen card.

4 Tell the audience that you need a card now. Perform another double lift to conceal the spectator's card as you actually show the audience the second of the two identical cards. Name this as your chosen card. Place the cards back on to the pack and place the pack on to the table.

5 Slide the top card (the spectator's card) off into your right hand, being careful not to reveal it to the audience, and place your hand down on the table, next to the spectator's.

6 Ask another member of the audience to tap three times on each of your hands. Tell the spectator to turn his hand over and reveal his card. You should do the same and the cards will appear to have swapped.

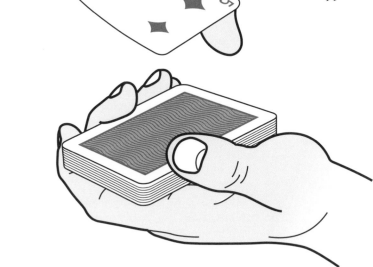

Chameleon Aces

Two black Aces are shown to the audience and placed in a spectator's hand. On turning them over, it is revealed that they have changed to red Aces and that the magician is, in fact, holding the black ones. You will need to have perfected the art of the double lift for this trick (see page 13). There is also a difficult manoeuvre towards the end of the trick, which is why it has a high skill level.

Skill level ♦♦♦♦♦

How to do it

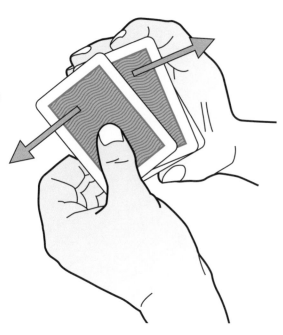

1 Fan through the pack of cards, removing all four Aces and set aside the rest of the pack. Arrange the Aces red, black, red, black.

2 Ask for a volunteer from the audience. Fan out the four cards, face up, in front of her then square up the pile.

3 Turn the cards face down and perform a double lift, revealing a black Ace to the audience. Return the cards to the pile and slide off the top card only, placing it face down in the spectator's hand.

4 Now slide the top card out of the way slightly and quickly slip out the two bottom cards (above). Make it look as if you're pulling off the top card and perform another double lift. Again, a black Ace will be visible. Return the cards to the top of the pile and slide off the real top card, another red Ace, and place in the spectator's hand.

5 You and the spectator now each hold two Aces. Everyone believes the spectator to be holding the black Aces and you to be holding the reds. You can now reveal that the opposite is true.

The Joker's having a laugh

A Joker is placed on the table and a spectator chooses any card from a fanned out pack. The spectator's card is placed back in the deck, face down, and the Joker is placed in the pack face up. The magician fans out the pack once again to reveal that the cards have reversed – the Joker is now face down and the spectator's card is face up.

Skill level ◆◆◆◆

You will need
A Joker.

How to do it

1 Show a Joker to your audience and place it face down on the table in front of you. Ask for a volunteer and pass her the pack to shuffle.

2 Take back the pack, fan out the cards (see page 11) and ask the spectator to pick one, memorize it and return it to the pack. Use the little finger of the hand holding the pack to make a subtle break above the spectator's card.

3 Subtly split the pack at the break and perform a false shuffle so that the spectator's card moves to the top of the pack (see page 10). It should appear as if you have squared up the pack, made a new cut and then shuffled the cards. You can perform any other shuffles you like, as long as the spectator's card remains on top.

4 Ask the spectator to show the card on the table to the audience. While she is doing this you need to hold the pack closely in your left hand and slide the top card slightly away from the pack with your right hand. Flick the pack over so that the pack is now face up with the spectator's card face down on top.

5 Split the pack, opening it just enough for a card to be inserted, moving the top half of the split slightly forwards as you do so to ensure the upturned cards are hidden, and ask the spectator to place the Joker face down in the pack.

6 Flip the pack back over so it is now face down again – apart from the spectator's card and the Joker. Now cut the deck twice so that the spectator's card moves within the pack. You need to make sure that the spectator's card comes fairly near the top of the pack, while the Joker stays nearer the bottom. This way, the audience will not spot the Joker as you riffle through the pack.

7 Riffle through the pack, closely, so the audience cannot glimpse the face-up cards and tell the audience that you are making the cards turn over.

8 Fan out the pack to reveal that the spectator's card is now face up in the face-down pack. Place it on the table; turn the pack over and fan through it again to find the Joker, which is now face down in the face-up pack.

Nimble fingers

A spectator chooses a card then shuffles it back into the pack. The magician fans through the deck to locate a 'rogue' card, which is handed to another spectator to make sure it stays out of trouble. The magician removes four other cards from the pack showing them, one by one, to the spectator, asking if each in turn is his card. None of them are, but when the magician goes through the cards again to double check, the last one turned over is the spectator's chosen card after all. This trick requires some good sleights of hand, which need to be executed with speed and confidence in order to fool the audience. If performed well this is very entertaining to watch.

Skill level ◆◆◆◆◆

How to do it

1 Shuffle the cards well in front of the audience, glimpsing the bottom card as you do so.

2 Holding the pack in your left hand, with your hand over the top of the pack start sliding off cards into your right hand one by one using your right thumb. Ask a volunteer to tell you to stop whenever he likes.

3 As you are sliding off the cards, gently loosen the bottom card of the pack away from the rest, holding it in place with the tips of your left thumb and fingers. The cards you are sliding off should give enough cover for you to be able to do this gradually over a number of cards (above).

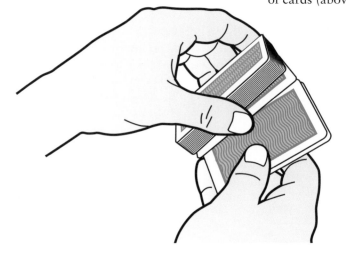

4 When the spectator tells you to stop, pretend to square up the pile of cards in your right hand but allow the main pack to hover over this pile and carefully drop the bottom card on top without the audience noticing. You now have the bottom card on top of this pile (left).

5 Put the main pack on the table and offer the pile of cards in your right hand to the spectator. Tell him to look at, and memorize, the top card, as this is the one he told you to stop at. Now give him all of the cards and tell him to shuffle his card back into the pack so that it is lost.

6 Next, you need to tell your audience that there is a rogue card in the pack that needs to be removed before it causes any trouble. Fan through the deck (see page 11), locate the spectator's card (the one that you memorized earlier) and count four cards to the left of it. Remove the fourth card (the rogue card) and hand it to another member of the audience to look after.

7 Keep a break in the pack where the rogue card came from – there should be three cards and then the spectator's card at the beginning of one section. Maintain the break with your little finger as you pretend to square up and cut the pack, moving the pile containing the spectator's card to the top of the deck. There should now be three random cards at the top of the deck, followed by the spectator's card.

8 Remove the top card, show it to the spectator and ask if this is his card. When he says it is not, put it back on the pack briefly then slide it off and place it face down on the table. Do this again with the next card.

9 When you get to the third card, show it to the spectator, replace it on the pack, but then slide out the card beneath it (the spectator's card) and place this on the table instead. Now show the fourth card and place that on the table as well.

10 Shake your head and tell the audience that you think the rogue card is still having an adverse effect on the pack. Ask the person holding it to insert it anywhere in the pack so that it is hidden and move the pack off the table somewhere.

11 Pick up the four cards – with the spectator's card second from top. Flip up the top card and ask if it is his. When he says no, place it back on the pile and carefully slide out the card beneath it (his). Place this on the table. Go through the other three cards in the same way until all four cards are on the table again, now with the spectator's at the bottom of the pile.

12 Pick up the pile one last time, flip over the cards and comment on how the trick has never gone wrong like this before, throwing each card face up on to the table as you do. Pause as you get to the final card then put it down a little more slowly and wait for the surprise to sink in as the spectator realizes that this is, at last, his card.

Top tip

As you go through the cards in step 11, it is possible that the audience might notice you have held up the same card twice when removing the spectator's card to the table. To avoid this, once you have removed his card, hold the remaining cards up together, as this is less likely to be spotted.

Crazy cards

A spectator chooses a card and the magician offers to swap another card for the spectator's. The original card is buried in the pack and the magician deals another to the spectator, showing her the card before placing it in front of her. He brushes the next card in the pack over this new card, which now appears in his hand.

Skill level ◆◆◆

How to do it

1 Shuffle the pack in front of your audience before you begin. Ask for a volunteer and tell her to select any card and hold on to it.

2 Tell her you want to exchange her card for a new one. Perform a double lift to reveal the second card from the top of the pack (see page 13). Put the cards back on top. Cut the pack and ask her to insert her card. Now slide off the top card from the pack and place it on the table face down in front of her – she will believe this to be the card she saw.

3 Perform another double lift and show her the card. Return the cards to the top of the pack and slide off the top card. Brush this over the spectator's card on the table and then show it to her. It will be the card she thought she had got in the exchange. At no point must the spectator look at her card.

4 Now you can do another double lift and announce another exchange. Give the spectator the top card once more and brush your card over hers. She will think her card has changed into the second card that she saw.

Top tip

For your audience to believe that you have placed the card that they have seen on the table you will need to be totally confident performing the double lift. Practise this skill until you have perfected it and remember to distract your audience by keeping up a convincing patter.

A flick of the wrist

A spectator chooses a card and returns it to the centre of the pack, which the magician then shuffles. The top card is removed and shown to the spectator but this is not her card. The magician places the same card on the table in front of the spectator. When she turns the card over, it is the one she chose after all.

How to do it

1 Shuffle the pack in front of your audience, fan out the cards (see page 11) and invite a volunteer to select any card and memorize it.

2 Square up the deck, make a cut and ask the spectator to replace her card. You need to keep this break, which you can do subtly by holding the pack face down in your left hand with your little finger pushed slightly over the cut.

3 Maintain the break as you cut the deck and perform a false shuffle to move the spectator's card to the top of the pack (see page 10). You can perform another false shuffle to make the shuffle more convincing.

4 Square up the pack and perform a double lift to reveal the second card down (see page 13). Ask the spectator if this is her card. When she confirms that it is not her card, place the cards back on the pack. Now slide off the top card (which actually is her card) and place it in front of her on the table.

5 Look confused and ask her if she is sure that the card on the table is not hers. When she says it is not, ask her to turn it over once more to check for a second time. When she turns over the card it will indeed be hers.

Making the set

The magician picks three cards from the pack and places them face down on the table. A spectator is then invited to pick another card. When all the cards are turned over, they are revealed to be the four Tens.

Skill level ♦♦

Preparation
Before you begin, place two Tens together a few cards in from the bottom of the pack (below).

How to do it

1 Shuffle the pack of cards in front of your audience, being careful not to move the two Tens (see page 12).

2 Now fan out the cards (see page 11) and remove all four Tens, placing them face down in front of you on the table. For the two that are together in the pack, you need to remove them as if they were one card – it is probably best not to remove them first (right).

3 Turn the pack face down and fan it out on a table in front of a spectator. Pick up the four cards and square them up. Ask the spectator to select any card from the fan and hand it to you. Place the chosen card face down on top of the other four cards.

4 Perform a double lift (see page 13) and show the audience that the spectator chose a Ten. Carefully place these cards face up on the table so it is not obvious that there are two cards. Now fan out the remaining three cards and turn them over to reveal that you chose the other Tens in the pack.

concealed card

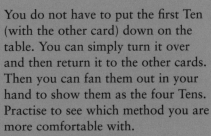

Top tip

You do not have to put the first Ten (with the other card) down on the table. You can simply turn it over and then return it to the other cards. Then you can fan them out in your hand to show them as the four Tens. Practise to see which method you are more comfortable with.

A sure sign

A spectator is asked to choose between two identical cards with different coloured backs. She signs the card and it is put in front of her. The magician brushes the other card over the top, and they have both miraculously changed colour. However, their signature remains intact on the card that was placed before the spectator. This is a trick that requires plenty of skill with sleights but it is a real showstopper!

Skill level ♦♦♦♦♦

You will need
Two duplicate cards: one the same colour as your main deck and one a different colour. A pen.

Preparation
If your regular pack is blue, you need to pick out one card and take the identical card from another blue pack and the same card from a red pack. With the cards face down, hold one blue-backed card in your left hand and hold the other two cards, as if they were one, in your right hand. The blue card should be under the red so it looks as if you are offering one blue and one red card.

How to do it
1 Offer the two cards to the spectator and ask her to choose her preferred colour and, depending on which she chooses, perform the trick as follows.

2 If she picks the blue card, put it on top of the other cards in your right hand and turn the pile face up. Pull off the top card – which the audience believes to be red – and place it, face up, on the table. It is actually the second blue card. Turn over the cards in your hand, as one, so that the audience sees the blue double. Now putting the cards face up in front of the spectator, ask her to sign the card. She thinks she is signing the blue card, when she is actually signing the red. You will need to keep a firm hold of the cards so that they do not separate and give the game away.

3 Place the blue card from the table under the double and put the top card on the table face up in front of the spectator. This is the red card with her signature on.

4 You now have the two blue cards face up in your left hand. Palm off the top card with your right hand (see page 14), distracting the attention of the audience by sliding the other card over the spectator's card on the table. Hide the palmed card behind your back or in a pocket.

5 Place the remaining card face up beside the spectator's card on the table and turn them both over. Her blue card has changed into a red one!

6 If the spectator chooses the red card, turn both cards face up and place the double on top of the single blue card. Ask her to sign the top card, which she believes to be the red one. It is actually blue. Once she has signed it, place the card face up on the table in front of her.

7 Turn the remaining cards over, as one, to confirm that you still have the blue card and that the spectator's must be the red one. Now you need to palm off the blue card and, at the same time, turn the red card over so that it is face up again and the audience cannot see the back. Slide the single card over the card on the table while you get rid of the palmed card.

8 Place your card on the table next to the spectator's and turn them both over – her red card has changed into a blue one.

Top tip

For this trick you need to be adept at double lifts and palming cards. It is also important to memorize the order of the steps required depending on whether the spectator chooses a red or blue card, so be sure of these before performing in front of your audience.

Don't bet on it

The magician deals out three piles of seven cards and asks a spectator to choose the top card of any pile, memorize it and return it. The magician then slaps the pile of cards and asks the spectator to point out the pile that contains his card. The spectator turns over the top card to discover that it is not his card after all – it has moved to a different pile. You will need to be good at palming a card before you perform this trick in front of an audience.

Skill level ♦♦

How to do it

1 Shuffle the pack of cards in front of your audience and ask for a volunteer. Ask if he would like to shuffle the pack as well.

2 Take the cards back and deal three piles on to the table, each containing seven cards. Ask the spectator to choose the top card of any pile, look at it and return it to the same pile.

3 Tell the audience that you are now going to slam each of the three piles to wake the cards up and get them to move around.

4 Slam the pile containing the spectator's card first. As you do so, palm his card into your hand (see page 14). Keeping your hand low over the cards so the audience cannot see the palmed card, slam one of the other piles and drop the palmed card on top (below). Slam the last pile for effect.

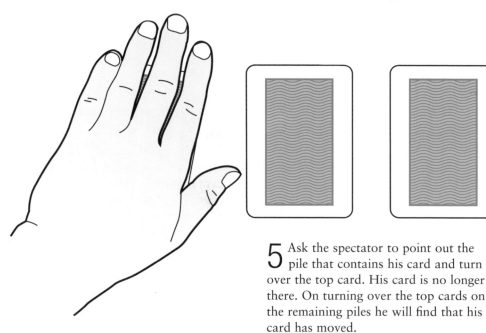

5 Ask the spectator to point out the pile that contains his card and turn over the top card. His card is no longer there. On turning over the top cards on the remaining piles he will find that his card has moved.

Top of the heap

The magician places the four Kings at the bottom of a shuffled pack. With a flick of the wrist the Kings miraculously move to the top. This trick takes a good deal of practice, and the more you practise, the more convincing it will be.

Skill level ♦♦♦

Preparation
Alternate the Kings with random cards at the top of the pack (random card, King, random card, King, random card, and so on). All cards should be face down.

How to do it
1 With the pack in your left hand, perform a double lift with your right hand, showing the first King (which in reality is the second card down) to the audience (see page 13). Put the cards on a table in front of you, placing them closer to you than to the audience, so they do not notice that there are two cards instead of one.

2 Repeat the double lift three more times so that the audience believes there are four Kings on the table. There should actually be eight cards with the Kings amongst them.

3 Place the pile of eight cards in your right hand and perform the double lift once more. Show the card(s) to the audience again, if you like, to confirm that it is just one King that you are holding. Now place the card(s) on top of the main pack and slide the top card to the bottom. The audience will believe that you have moved the King to the bottom of the pack.

4 Repeat this three more times, until all the Kings are now together at the top of the pack.

5 Taking the pack in your left hand, riffle through it with your right then square it up and deal the top four cards, face up, on to the table. The four Kings have managed to move back to the top of the pack.

Top tip

It is easier to conceal the fact that there are eight cards instead of four if you hold the pile in your right hand when putting them back on the pack. Obviously this looks a little clumsy, as you will have to break to slide each card with the remaining cards in your hand. However, with practice, you should be able to find your own way of doing this comfortably.

The cards keep moving

A spectator chooses a card and returns it anywhere in the pack. The magician taps the pack and tells the spectator that her card has moved to the top of the deck. When the card is turned over, however, it is not her card. The magician puts the card face down on the table and then pulls the same card from his pocket. When the spectator looks again, the card appears to have changed into her original card. This is a great trick that requires a little practice to perform really well.

Skill level ◆◆◆◆

How to do it

1 Shuffle the pack in front of your audience and ask for a volunteer.

2 Fan out the pack (see page 11) and ask the spectator to select any card, memorize it and return it wherever she wishes. As she is putting the card back, make a break with the little finger of the hand holding the pack.

3 Maintain the break as you pretend to square up and split the pack for a shuffle, with the spectator's card on top of the left pile. Perform a false shuffle to bring the spectator's card to the top of the pack (see page 10). You can perform another false shuffle to make the move more convincing, if you like, but make sure you keep the spectator's card at the top of the pack.

4 Now place the pack on the table, tap it and tell the audience that the spectator's card will jump to the top of the pack.

5 Picking up the pack, perform a double lift, to show the audience the second card (see page 13). The audience will believe this is the top card and that you have got the trick wrong. Put the card(s) back on the pack and slide off the top card (the spectator's card), placing it on the table in front of her. You can look a bit confused and say that this happens sometimes, as the card jumps a bit too far.

6 Now you need to palm the top card of the pack (the card the spectator thinks is in front of her) and put your hand in your pocket (see page 14). You then pretend that you are pulling the card out of your pocket. Show it to the spectator – it is the card she thought was on the table (below).

7 Now ask the spectator to turn over the card on the table and it will be the card that she chose at the beginning of the trick.

Top tip

Keep the pack as close to your body as possible when palming the card. Chat to the audience to distract them from what you are doing. Make sure you keep your hand facing away from them and then just slide it into your pocket. Wear something with big pockets that are easy to get into!

Your eyes deceive you

The magician fans out the pack and asks a volunteer to pick a card and then return it to the top of the deck. When the magician peels off the top card and shows it to the spectator, it is not his chosen card after all – his card has disappeared.

Skill level ♦♦

How to do it

1 Shuffle the pack in front of your audience and ask for a volunteer.

2 Fan out the pack (see page 11) and ask the spectator to remove any card, show it to the rest of the audience and then memorize it. While he is doing this, square up the pack and palm off the top card (see page 14).

3 Ask the spectator to place his card on the top of the pack. Pretend to square up the pack once again, returning the palmed card to the top of the deck as you do so.

4 Place the pack on the table and ask the spectator to reveal the identity of his card. When he has done this ask him to turn over the top card. He will be more than a little surprised to see that it is not his card at all, but a completely different one.

Second time lucky

A spectator chooses and memorizes a card before replacing it anywhere in the pack. The magician then asks the spectator to deal off a number of cards – specified by a second volunteer – on to the table. The last card is dealt face up, as this should be the spectator's card. When it is not the correct card the magician announces that he will try and, sure enough, on recounting the cards from the pack, the last card is the spectator's.

Skill level ♦♦

How to do it

1 Shuffle the pack in front of your audience and ask for a volunteer.

2 Fan out the pack (see page 11) and ask the spectator to choose and remove any card. He must then memorize the card and return it anywhere in the pack.

3 Use the little finger of the hand holding the pack to keep a break above the spectator's card. Square up the cards, retaining the break in such a way that the audience cannot see.

4 Now cut the pack at the break. The spectator's card should be the top card of the bottom section. Finish the cut so that the spectator's card is at the top of the reassembled pack. Perform a false shuffle, if you like, keeping the spectator's card at the top (see page 9). Place the pack on the table.

5 Tell the spectator that the audience is going to help him to locate his card. Ask another member of the audience to pick a number between one and 30. The spectator must now deal off that many cards face down on to the table. When he reaches the last card, he must flip it over and it should be his.

6 Of course the last card is not his, and you can now tell the audience that you will put your magician's powers to the test and have a go yourself. Return the dealt cards to the top of the pack and count off the required number of cards once more. The spectator's card is now the correct number of cards into the pack as is revealed when you flip over the last card to prove your skills.

Throwing a tantrum

A spectator picks a card from a fanned out pack then memorizes and returns it. The magician shuffles the pack and the spectator is allowed three chances to try and find his chosen card. None of the cards are correct but the magician says he thinks he can make the card appear. He takes the three cards in his hand and taps them – two cards fall away on to the table and the remaining card is the one chosen by the spectator at the beginning of the trick. This trick requires plenty of practice as there are various sleights of hand to perform and authenticity depends on your speed. Despite this, the trick is easy once mastered and will astound the audience every time.

Skill level ♦♦♦♦♦

How to do it

1 Shuffle the pack in front of your audience and ask for a volunteer. See if he would like to shuffle the pack as well then ask him to return it to you.

2 Fan out the cards in front of the spectator (see page 11) and ask him to remove one and memorize it, showing it to the rest of the audience as well.

3 While he is doing this, separate the bottom three cards slightly from the rest of the pack in such a way that the audience cannot see.

Top tip

The success of this trick relies on your acting skills as you will have to make your audience believe that you have messed up the trick, right until the last minute when you reveal the chosen card.

4 As the spectator replaces his card you must quickly cut the deck twice. He will place his card in the centre of the pack and this will be the first cut. Place the top section on the table (it should have the spectator's card at the bottom). Now cut again, this time leaving the three bottom cards at the break. You now have three piles of cards. Reassemble the pack, placing the pile with the spectator's on top of the pile with three cards. Put the third pile on top of this.

5 You can now perform a false shuffle, if you like, to convince your audience that you have not placed the card in the deck. Remember to keep the bottom four cards in place (see page 12). Square up the pack and tell your spectator that he has three chances to spot his card. Turn the pack over, show him the bottom card of the pack and ask if it is his. When he says 'No', turn the pack face down and slide the bottom card out and on to the table. Slide the next card out and move it to the top of the pack.

6 Again, turn the pack face up and
show the spectator the next card.
When he confirms that this is not his
card either, turn the pack face down
again and carefully shift this card back
a little with your fingers and slide out
the card above it, which is actually the
chosen card (right). Place this on top of
the card on the table then remove the
next card (the one you actually showed)
and put this on top of the pack.

7 Now it is the last chance for the right
card to appear and the spectator will
be expecting to see his card at this point,
thinking this is the climax of the trick.
So, again, show the bottom card of the
pack and when he confirms that it is not
his card, slide it out to join the other two
on the table. Slide out the next card and
place it on top of the pack.

8 You should now have three face-
down cards on the table, with the
spectator's card in the middle. Turn the
trio face up and show the spectator the
bottom card once more, saying 'Are you
sure this is not your card?'. When he
confirms it is not, shake your head and
look disappointed. While you are doing
this, square up the pile in such a way
that the top and bottom cards are
held firmly between your thumb and
forefinger and the middle card is a little
loose. Motion that you are going to
throw the cards on to the table in
disgust, then flick the cards, face up and
only the middle card will fall – the
spectator's chosen card (right)!

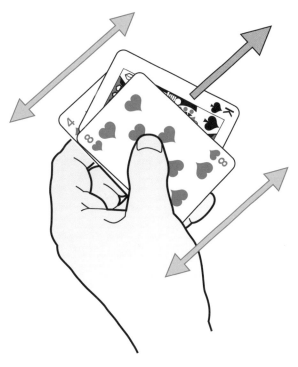

Jack catcher

A spectator is given a black Jack and asked to put it back in the pack. The magician shuffles the pack then cuts it and, on fanning out the cards, the spectator's black Jack is face up between the two face-down red Jacks.

Skill level ◆◆◆

Preparation
Before you perform the trick, you need to put one red Jack at the top of the pack and the other at the bottom. All cards should be face down.

How to do it
1 Perform a false shuffle, keeping the top and bottom cards in place (see pages 9–10). Ask for a volunteer. Fan through the pack and tell the spectator that you are picking out one of the black Jacks for her. When you have located one, hand it to her.

2 Turn the pack face down, fan out the cards and ask the spectator to return her Jack to the pack, anywhere she likes. You need to make a break in the pack underneath her card as she does so.

3 Keeping the break, pretend to square up the pack and make a cut. As you are moving the top section underneath the bottom section, take hold of the spectator's Jack with the thumb and fingers of your left hand, twist the other cards at an angle away from the audience and flip the Jack so that it is now face up. You then need to complete the cut quickly so that the spectator's Jack is now face up between the two red Jacks (below).

4 With the pack face down, fan out the cards in front of the audience. There will be one card face up and this is the spectator's black Jack. Turn over the cards to either side to reveal that the card is surrounded by the red Jacks.

Mind over matter

The tricks in this section do not rely on clever trickery or well-practised sleights of hand for success, but rather on the magician's ability to convince an audience that he has been blessed with psychic powers. The skill required here is not so much lightness of touch as creating a credible persona and really playing the part. Performed with a little panache, even the simplest tricks can leave an audience completely spellbound and certain that you must indeed have an insight beyond their wildest expectations.

Feeling the vibes

A spectator deals two equal piles of as many cards as he likes, discarding the rest of the pack. He then cuts one of the piles, looks at the bottom card of the cut and places the cut cards on top of the untouched pile. The magician fans through all the cards and effortlessly picks out the spectator's card.

Skill level ◆

How to do it

1 Ask a spectator to shuffle the pack and deal as many cards as he wants into two piles, with an equal number of cards in each. It is important that you count the number of cards in each pile. The spectator can set aside the remainder of the pack.

2 Now ask the spectator to choose one of the two piles and cut it wherever he likes, memorizing the bottom card of the cut before placing the cut cards on top of the untouched pile. The spectator should put the remaining cut cards on top of those.

3 The spectator has unwittingly placed his card at the centre of the pile. Assuming he dealt eight cards into each pile, you will know that his card is the eighth one from the top.

4 Fan the cards out in front of you, with the backs of the cards facing you (see page 11). Starting at your right, pretend to feel each card to determine whether or not it is the spectator's. Simply count along as you go (below).

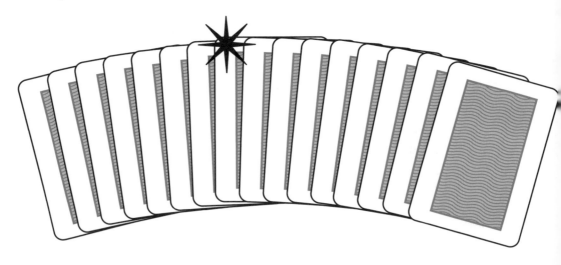

Psychic powers

A spectator thinks of any card and keeps it in his mind. The magician flicks through the pack and extracts a card but it is not the card the spectator was thinking of. The spectator then locates his card and moves it to the top of the pack. The pack is cut and shuffled and the magician finds the card.

Skill level ◆◆

How to do it

1 Ask for a volunteer and tell him to think of any card in the pack.

2 Shuffle the pack in front of the audience and begin counting cards face up on to the table, pretending to be looking for the spectator's card. When you reach the twenty-sixth card, hold it up and ask the spectator if this is his card – of course it won't be (unless you are incredibly lucky!). Remember the card and put it back on top of the pack. Place the other twenty-five cards that you counted out back on top of the pack too.

3 Now hand the pack to the spectator and ask him to fan through and remove his card, being careful not to reveal it to you. Ask him to place the card on top of the pack and tell him to remove about one-third of the cards from the bottom of the pack and place them on top of his card.

4 Take the pack of cards back from the spectator and fan it out with the cards facing you (see page 11). Ask the spectator to concentrate hard on his chosen card and you will try to locate it. First you need to locate your card, which will be closer to the right end of the pack. Starting with the next card, count up to twenty-six. The twenty-sixth card will be the spectator's chosen card.

Fool's gold

The pack is shuffled and the magician chooses a card. He then asks the spectator a series of simple questions and she is able to guess the card. This is not a trick but a mind game. Basically, you are telling the spectator what the chosen card is, while making it look as if she has guessed it completely at random.

Skill level ♦

How to do it

1 Shuffle the pack and ask if the spectator wants to shuffle as well to make sure you are not hiding anything. Square up the pack, look at the top card and memorize it. Place the card face down on the table between you and the spectator and move the rest of the pack to the side.

2 Assuming that the card is the Four of Spades, ask the spectator to choose between red and black. If she chooses black, say she has made a good choice. If she says red, then say something like 'OK so that leaves us with the black cards'. (Obviously you need to alter this according to which card the spectator is actually guessing.)

3 Now ask her which suit she prefers – in this case Spades or Clubs. Again, accept this suit or pick the other, depending on what her response is.

4 You now have the correct suit and need to get the spectator to guess the right number. Ask which she would choose – the cards running from Ace to Seven or those running from Eight to King. Again keep the selection or eliminate it depending on her reply.

5 Now ask her to pick her favourite three cards from whichever set you have kept. If her selection doesn't contain the card, again eliminate these and you will be left with a possible four cards to choose from. If she has included it in her choice, you will be left with three. Whichever happens, you can now ask her to pick her favourite and repeat the process until you are left with just one card. Turn the card on the table over and it will be the same.

Upwardly mobile

A member of the audience chooses a card from the pack and shows it to the magician who tells her that he has a psychic friend who will be able to verify the chosen card over the telephone. The magician calls his friend, passes him over to the doubting spectator and, sure enough, the friend reveals the chosen card.

Skill level ♦

You will need
A mobile phone. An accomplice.

Preparation
Brief your friend in advance to make sure that he will be around at the appropriate time to take your call.

How to do it

1 Shuffle the pack well to prove that the cards are not in any particular order before the trick commences.

2 Fan out the pack face down in front of the spectator (see page 11) and ask her to pick a card. When she has chosen, set aside the remaining cards and ask the spectator to turn her card over and place it in the centre of the table.

3 Call your friend. As soon as he answers, he needs to begin slowly naming each of the four suits. When he names the correct one – say Hearts – you say 'Hello'. He must then start going through the numbers and, this time, when he reaches the correct one you say, 'I'll just pass you over', or something similar. Your friend now knows the identity of the chosen card.

4 Pass the phone to the spectator and witness her amazement as your friend reveals the identity of the card.

Top tips

- Use a mobile phone and not a landline so that your accomplice will be able to see that it is you calling and can start going through the suits immediately.

- Practise the trick a couple of times before you try this on an audience. Your timing needs to be perfect and your accomplice should not go through the cards too slowly – the long gaps may give the game away.

Vanished

The magician deals out six cards and asks a spectator to memorize one of them. The magician then places the cards back on the pack and says that the chosen card is going to vanish within the pack. On placing the, now, five cards on the table, the spectator sees that his card is definitely missing. This trick is really easy and works by mimicking the way in which the human brain operates.

Preparation

First you need to prepare your deck. Remove the Jacks, Queens and three of the Kings from the pack, leaving one black King in the pack, and arrange the cards in two rows – one with six cards and one with five. The first row will be red Queen, black Jack, red Jack, black King, red King, black Queen and the second row will be red Queen, black Jack, red Jack, black Queen, red King. Gather up the cards into their two separate piles so that the card on the left is at the bottom of the face-up pile in each case. Turn the piles face down and place the five-card pile at the bottom of the main deck of cards. Place this in the centre of the table.

How to do it

1 Ask for a volunteer. Deal out the pile of six cards face up in a row, starting to your left. Ask the spectator to choose and memorize one of the cards, without touching it.

2 Quickly gather up the cards and place the pile on top of the main deck. Tell the spectator to concentrate hard on his card while you try to guess it and make it disappear into the pack.

3 With the cards behind your back, count off the bottom five and move them to the top of the pack. Bring the deck out in front of your audience again.

4 Tell them that the spectator's card has now vanished into the pack. Count off the five cards into a pile and set aside the rest of the pack. Again starting to your left, turn the cards over one at a time. Sure enough, the spectator's card is no longer there.

Top tip

When you ask the spectator to pick and concentrate on just one card, the other cards will just become a background blur. As the other five cards look very similar he will not notice that they are not the same cards – he will just see that his is missing. However, you need to make sure that the first six cards are not on the table for very long. Tell the spectator that you want him to memorize one card as you are dealing them, then you can gather the cards up quickly afterwards.

Passing the power

The magician's assistant leaves the room while the magician asks a spectator to pick any nine playing cards from a fanned out pack. The magician lays the cards out on the table and asks the spectator to select and memorize any one card, which she indicates to everyone by touching it. The assistant is called back into the room and he is able to use his mind-reading powers to select the correct card. It is best to practise this trick a couple of times with your assistant before performing it in front of an audience.

Skill level ♦♦

You will need
An assistant.

How to do it

1 Ask your assistant to leave the room and tell the audience that he has special mind-reading powers that you are going to demonstrate with this trick.

2 Shuffle the pack and ask for a volunteer. Fan out the cards face down (see page 11) and ask the spectator to remove any nine cards. Turn the nine cards face up and arrange them on the table in three rows of three. Pick up the remaining cards and hold them in your left hand.

3 Ask the spectator to point to any of the nine cards. Now you can call your assistant back in.

4 Have the remaining pack in your left hand pointing towards the assistant and use your left thumb to indicate which is the chosen card. Just imagine the card as a replica of the nine cards on the table and then point your thumb to the bottom left, centre right and so on, depending on which card the spectator chose on the table (right).

Top tip

You don't want the audience to realize that you are using the pack of cards to indicate the chosen card so you or your assistant might want to keep talking as a distraction while the choosing process is going on.

Making a point

Eight cards are laid out on the table. The magician turns his back and a spectator chooses a card. The magician's assistant then points to various cards and the magician is able to tell her which one the spectator chose. This is another trick that requires an assistant and it would make a good follow-up to the previous trick (Passing the Power). On this occasion you guess the card.

Skill level ♦

You will need

An assistant.

Preparation

Before you begin make sure that there is an Eight among the first eight cards of the pack.

How to do it

1 Deal off eight cards face up into a pile on the table. Now arrange them according to the pattern that appears on an Eight card but do not make it obvious that this is what you are doing. It does not matter where the Eight card goes in the pattern.

2 Ask for a volunteer. Turn your back to the audience and tell the spectator to point to any one of the cards. When he has done this you can turn back.

3 Now your assistant points to different cards. At some point she must point to the Eight and when she does so, she will touch the symbol on the card that reflects the position of the spectator's card on the table. You now know where the card is and when she touches that card you can reveal that it is the spectator's (right).

Incredible card location

A spectator selects a card and replaces it in the pack. The pack is then cut and shuffled before being fanned out, face up, on the table. The magician tells the audience that he is going to memorize the deck order. He then turns around while the spectator moves her selected card to a different place in the pack. The magician turns back and is able to pick out the spectator's card as the one card that has been moved. This trick takes a bit of concentration but the amazing results make it worth the effort.

Skill level ♦♦♦♦

How to do it

1 Shuffle the pack in front of your audience. You need to know the identity of the top and bottom cards. The best way to do this without being detected is to glimpse the bottom card, shuffle it to the top (see page 10) and then glimpse the new bottom card – commit these to memory as the trick depends on them!

2 Ask for a volunteer, fan out the pack and ask her to select and memorize any card. Square up the pack and ask the spectator to return her card to the top of the deck. Cut the pack twice, finishing the cuts each time by placing the top pile underneath.

3 Now fan out the deck face up on the table and tell your audience that you are memorizing the location of all the cards in the pack so that you will be able to pick out any card that has changed position (below).

4 Locate your two memorized cards and then memorize the cards that are now between them. If you are lucky this will be just one – the spectator's card. If not, you need to know all of them to complete the trick successfully.

5 When you are ready, turn your back to your audience and ask the spectator to remove her card and replace it somewhere else in the pack.

6 Turn back and once again locate your two cards – the card that is missing from between them is the spectator's card. Pull it out, telling the audience that you know this is the only card that has changed position so it must be the spectator's chosen card.

Top tip

It doesn't really matter how long you take to memorize the cards. In fact, by taking a little longer to do so, you are more likely to convince your audience that you are indeed trying to memorize the exact location of all the cards in the pack.

Subliminal card prediction

The magician chooses a card from the pack and tells the spectator that she will be able to find the two cards that denote the number and suit of the chosen card. After dealing the cards into two piles the spectator removes the top card from each pile and sure enough, they are the same suit and number as the magician's card.

Skill level ◆◆

How to do it

1 Fan out the pack so that it is face up towards you and tell the audience that you are going to pick out a card. Look at the first two cards on the left of the fan. You need to find the card that matches the number value of the first card and the suit of the second. So, for example, if the first card is the Queen of Hearts and the second is the Five of Diamonds then you are looking for the Queen of Diamonds (below).

2 Remove the card from the pack and place it face down on the table. Ask for a volunteer. Square up the pack, turn it face down and hand it to the spectator. Tell her to deal off as many cards as she likes, face down, into a pile on the table.

3 Tell her to set aside the remaining cards and pick up the dealt pile. She needs to deal the cards into two separate piles, dealing alternately and face down, starting with the left.

4 You can now turn over your card and tell the spectator that you think you have been able to tell her, telepathically, the suit and value of your card. Tell her to turn over the top card on each of the two piles and they will indeed correspond to the suit and value of your card.

Mathematical miracles

All of the tricks in this section rely to some extent on mental agility and good concentration so, if maths is a strong point, they will prove fun and satisfying to perform. From the simplest numbers game to more complex card-counting acts, these mathematical miracles will have an audience demanding repeats as they try to figure out how they have been duped. And if maths is not a favourite subject, do not fear, as there are a good number of self-working tricks that can be performed with the minimum of advance pack preparation.

The card calendar

A spectator chooses a card and replaces it on top of the pack. He then cuts the pack three or four times to lose the card. The magician deals off cards according to the weeks and months in a year. On finishing, he turns over the top card of the pack to reveal that it is the spectator's card.

Skill level ♦♦

You will need
A Joker.

Preparation
Before you perform the trick you need to place the Joker at the bottom of the face-down pack.

How to do it

1 Shuffle the pack in front of your audience, being careful to keep the Joker at the bottom (see page 10). Ask for a volunteer. Fan out the pack and ask him to select a card and memorize it. Square up the pack and ask the spectator to replace his card on top.

2 Place the cards on the table and tell the spectator that he can cut the pack a number of times, if he likes, to ensure that his card is lost.

3 Tell the spectator that you forgot the Joker was in the pack and that it needs to be at the bottom. Fan through the pack until you find the Joker – the spectator's card will be directly to the right of it (below). You need to get the spectator's card to the top of the pack. The best way to do this is to separate the pack where the Joker is and square up the other section so that the spectator cannot see his card. Then, with both sections face up, place the pile with the Joker on top of the other pile and flip the whole pack over. Now the Joker is on the bottom and the spectator's card is on top of the pack.

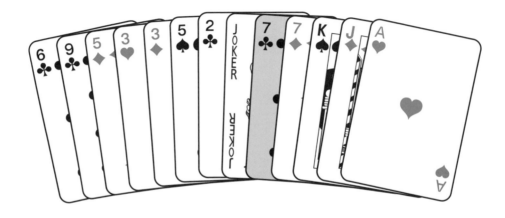

4 Now tell the spectator that you're going to attempt to find his card by using the card calendar. Say there are fifty-two weeks in the year and deal five cards from the pack on to the table into a pile and then deal two cards into another pile next to them. Now put the two cards on top of the five and then put the whole lot, face down, back on top of the face-down pack.

5 Next, state that there are twelve months in the year and deal twelve cards into a pile on the table. Square up the pile and place them back on top of the main pack.

6 Finally, state that there are seven days in a week and deal seven cards on to the table then pick them up and put them back on top of the pack.

7 The spectator's card will be the second card from the top. Square up the pack and perform a double lift, to reveal his card (see page 13).

Top tip

You need to be sure of the order of the steps in this trick for it to work. Practise on your own until you can deal out the cards easily while talking to an audience at the same time.

Crazy card prediction

The magician deals half the pack on to the table and then starts dealing this into three separate piles. Depending on the value of the first card in each pile, more are added until the magician is able to identify the next card to be dealt from the pack. This trick will really show off your mathematical and memory skills and it is best to practise on your own a few times before doing this in front of an audience.

Skill level ♦♦♦

How to do it

1 Shuffle the pack well in front of your audience and deal off half the pack, face up, on to the table in front of you. Memorize the fourth card that you deal. Once you have reached twenty-six cards, put the other half to one side, square up the dealt pile and turn it face down.

2 Tell your audience that you are going to make three piles of cards on the table, each of which must have a value of ten or above. Deal three cards, face up, each the beginning of a separate pile. Swap the cards in your hand for the pile you set aside earlier, but do not mention this to the audience: just do it naturally.

3 You now need to bring the value of each pile to ten. So, for example, if the first dealt card is a Six, add four cards to it. If the next is a Seven, add three cards, and so on. You place these cards face down, on top of the face-up card (below). If any of the piles has a picture card or Ace, you do not need to add any more cards.

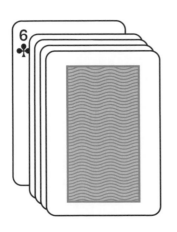 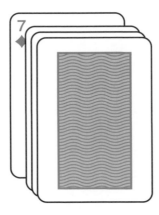 

4 When all the cards have a value of ten or more, place the pile of cards that you are holding on top of the original pile and, in your head, add up the number of face-down cards that you have placed. Subtract this from number 26.

5 Hand the pack of cards to a member of the audience and ask her to deal out that number of cards, face down, on to the table. Now tell your audience that you are able to predict the value of the next card to be dealt from the pack. To add to the mystery, turn over the top face-down cards from any of the piles on the table and dwell on them for a few seconds, as if performing some complicated calculation.

6 Tell the audience your prediction (it will be the card that you memorized at the beginning of the trick) and ask the spectator to go ahead and deal the next card from the pack. Your prediction will be correct.

Top tip

This trick sounds more complicated than it is. Go through the instructions slowly and get a feel for the order of the steps before you try performing it in front of an audience.

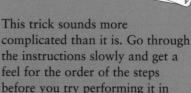

A numbers game

A pack of cards is divided into suits then stacked together. The pack is cut randomly on nine separate occasions and the cards are then dealt into 13 piles. On turning over the piles, it is revealed that each contains four cards of the same rank. This is a self-working trick which is impressive and quite easy to master, just as long as you make sure you follow the instructions carefully.

Skill level ♦♦

How to do it

1 Divide a pack of playing cards into the four suits and arrange each suit face up on the table in numerical order from Ace at the bottom through to the King at the top (below).

2 Place the piles on top of each other, alternating between red and black then turn the pack over so the cards are face down.

3 Peel off the top 21 cards from the pack, turning each card face up before you place it on the table so that the cards remain in the same order (this is very important!). Square up the pile, turn it over so the cards are face down again, and place this pile of cards under the remaining pile.

4 Ask a member of the audience to cut the pack wherever he likes nine times. Remember that he needs to move the bottom pile to the top after each cut.

5 Next you need to deal the pack into 13 piles, going in the same direction each round, so that you end up with four cards in each pile.

6 Now it is time to turn over each of the 13 piles to reveal to your astounded audience that the pack of cards has been split very neatly into the 13 ranks of the deck – each of the piles containing the same card from each of the four suits.

Top tip

It is important that you do not lose your concentration at all during this trick. It is impressive but given that there are a number of different elements it would be a shame to go through the whole trick only for it not to work at the very end.

Calling the shots

With his back to the audience, the magician instructs a spectator to pick any card from the pack. The spectator is then instructed to deal out cards from the pack and the magician is able to stop her when she has reached her chosen card. This is an easy trick to master yet one that is quite impressive. You do not even touch the cards so your audience will be really baffled as to how it works.

Skill level ♦

How to do it

1 Turn your back to the audience right from the beginning to add to the suspense. Ask for a volunteer and tell her to shuffle the pack to her satisfaction. Next, ask her to pick any non-picture card from the pack, memorize it and place it on top of the other cards.

2 Tell the spectator to take the value of her card and to count this many cards from the bottom of the pack, placing them back on top of the pack. So, for example, if her chosen card was a Nine, she must move nine cards.

3 Now tell the spectator to deal the cards, face up on the table, from the top of the pack. As each card is placed on the table, ask her to call out its value and suit.

4 In working out the chosen card, discount the first card that is dealt and called out. From the second card onwards begin to count, starting at one. When the spectator calls out a card that has the same number value as the number of cards you have counted, this will be her card. So, if she calls out a Nine of Hearts and you are on nine, that is the one.

Top tip

There is a possibility that there will be two or more cards that match the number you have counted to. This will not ruin the trick as there is still a good chance that the first one you guess will be correct. If it is not then just go with the other one and your audience will still be impressed.

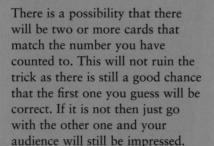

It all adds up

A member of the audience chooses two cards from the pack at random. The magician asks her to do some simple maths and is then able to reveal the values of the cards she picked.

Skill level ♦

Preparation

Before you begin this trick, you need to remove every picture card and every Ten from the pack.

How to do it

1 Ask a member of the audience to shuffle the pack and then take it back from her. Fan the cards out on the table in front of the spectator and ask her to choose any card and memorize the number before returning it to the pack.

2 Inform the spectator that some concentration is required, as she will need to do a little mental arithmetic. First, she must multiply the number of the card by two. Next she should add five and finally she must multiply the total by five.

3 Ask her to pick a second random card and add that number to the total she has reached already. She can then tell you the final number. In order to calculate her two cards, all you do is subtract 25 from the number she tells you. The resulting digits are the values of the two cards that were chosen. So, for example, if she says '64', you mentally subtract 25 which leaves you with 39. The two cards were therefore a Three and a Nine.

Clever guesswork

The magician deals 21 cards from the pack. He hands the cards to a spectator and tells him to pick a number between one and ten and then count off that many cards. The magician then deals the remaining cards out, counts along the number that the spectator discarded and is able to identify the next card in the row.

Skill level ♦♦

Preparation
Before you perform the trick, choose any card from the pack, memorize it, and place it face down tenth from the top of the pack.

How to do it

1 Ask for a volunteer. Tell him that you are going to take the top 21 cards from the pack. Keep the cards in the same order as you count them off. Hand the pile of cards to the spectator and set aside the rest of the pack. Tell the spectator that you're going to predict the identity of a card.

2 Turn your back to the audience and tell the spectator to think of a number between one and ten and to remove that many cards from the top of the pile. This will indicate the card that you are going to predict at the end of the trick.

3 Turn back to the audience and take the remaining cards back from the spectator. Starting to your left, deal out ten cards in a row, keeping them face down. Next ask the spectator how many cards he took from the pile. If he took eight, you then need to count in eight cards from the right of the row. The next card will be the card you memorized.

4 Push this card forward from the others and tell the spectator that he randomly selected this card because he counted off eight from his pile and this was the next in the row. Announce your prediction and ask the spectator to turn the card over to reveal you are correct.

Who can't count ?

The magician counts eight cards out on to the table then asks a spectator to check them. The magician says he thought he saw nine cards and when he recounts them there are indeed nine. He then asks the spectator to confirm this but when he counts, there are now ten cards. The magician counts once more and the number has increased to eleven. The spectator recounts and it has gone up again, to twelve!

Skill level ◆◆◆◆

How to do it

1 Shuffle the pack and deal eight cards on to the table. Ask a spectator to recount the dealt cards to confirm that there are eight of them. While he is concentrating on this, palm two cards from the top of the remaining pack into your hand (see page 14 and below).

2 When the spectator says that there are indeed eight cards, look confused and say that you were sure you saw him count nine.

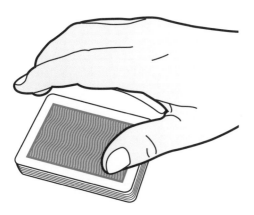

3 Take the pile from the spectator with the hand containing the palmed cards, placing your whole hand over the pile and sliding it towards you across the table. Drop the palmed cards on top of the pile as you do this.

4 Now recount the cards on to the table but count the final two cards together so that your new total comes to nine (although there are actually now ten cards in the pile).

5 Remark on how strange that is and ask the spectator to count again, just to make sure you have got it right this time. As he is counting palm another two cards into your hand from the main pack. He will count off ten cards and again you need to say that you think you might have seen eleven cards there.

6 Repeat the process, placing the palmed cards on top of the pile and, once again, count out the cards keeping the last two together. You will count eleven cards.

7 Ask the spectator to do another recount, being especially careful this time. Of course they will now count twelve cards.

Spell it out

A spectator chooses nine cards from the pack and shuffles them. While the magician's back is turned the spectator pulls out the third card from the top of the pile and shows it to the rest of the audience before returning it to the same place. The spectator then silently spells the name of the card, dealing a card on to the table for each letter. At the end of every word, the cards are replaced on the pack. When the card has been spelt, the pile is given back to the magician who puts them behind his back and is able to pull out the chosen card. The success of this trick depends on the spectator as much as it does on the magician so make sure you are very clear with your instructions.

Skill level ♦♦

How to do it

1 Hand the pack of cards to a willing spectator and tell her to pick out any nine cards of her choice, discarding the rest of the pack.

2 Turn your back to the audience and instruct the spectator to shuffle the pile of cards, then fan them out face down and remove the third card from the top. She should memorize this card and show it to the audience before replacing it in the same place in the fan and squaring up the pile.

3 Tell the spectator to think of the card and then silently spell it out, dealing off cards to indicate each letter. The card will have three separate words to its name (something of something) and she must deal cards on to the table, one word at a time. So, for example, if her card was the Jack of Diamonds, she will be begin by silently spelling out 'J-A-C-K', placing one card face down on to the table for every letter, the next card being placed on top of the last. When the word has been spelt, those cards are collected up, placed underneath the other cards and the next word is spelt out in the same way.

  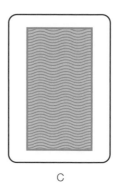 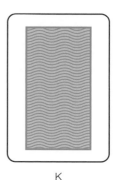

J   A   C   K

4 Once the whole card has been spelt and the pile squared up once more, you can turn back to face the audience and take the cards. Put them behind your back and tell your audience that you are now going to sense with your hands which card was picked earlier. The card will be the one in middle of the pile, so you just need to count four cards from one hand to the other and the chosen card will be the fifth.

5 Keep this card in one hand and discard the remaining cards. Ask the spectator what her card was and bring out the card that you are holding. All being well, it will be the card she chose.

Top tip

Double check at each stage of the trick that your volunteer understands what she has to do or it will not work.

Three stragglers

Three members of the audience each select and memorize a card. The remaining cards are dealt into three piles with each spectator placing his card on a pile and performing a cut. The pack is then dealt into two piles – one face up and one face down – until all the cards have been used. When the spectators do not see their cards in the face-up pile, the pile is discarded and the process repeated. Eventually there are only three cards left and, on turning them over, the magician reveals them to be those of the spectators. This is a great trick that requires some basic calculations and a quick pace to keep your audience intrigued. It works all by itself as long as you stick to the instructions given.

Skill level ♦♦♦

How to do it

1 Shuffle the pack of cards in front of your audience, fan them out face down and ask three volunteers to each pick and memorize a card.

2 Shuffle the pack again if you like, then deal out the cards into three piles – the first containing ten cards and the second and third each containing 15 cards. You will have nine cards left, which you hold on to for now.

3 Ask the first spectator to place his card, face down, on top of the first pile and then to make a cut from the second pile and place the cut portion on top of the first pile.

4 Now ask the next spectator to do the same, but with the second pile of cards. (So, place his card on the second pile, make a cut from the third and place those cards on top of the second pile.)

5 The third person will place his card on the third pile. There are no piles of cards left to make a cut from, so ask the spectator to use the nine remaining cards that you are holding and place those on top of this pile.

6 Next you need to put the last pile of cards on top of the middle pile and then stack this pile on top of the first pile. Remove the four top cards from the pack and place them underneath.

7 The next part of the trick is easy, but if you have made any mistakes up until now, it will not work. Square up the pack and hold it face down. Deal the cards into two piles on the table – one face up and one face down. Begin with a face up card and continue until all the cards have been dealt. Ask the spectators to shout when they see one of their cards. The trick is that this will not happen, as all of their cards should be in the face-down pile.

8 When you get to the end of the pack and none of the chosen cards have been seen, push the face-up pile to one side and repeat the process with the remaining cards, dealing two piles and telling the spectators to let you know when they spot one of their cards. Again it will not happen.

9 Eventually, after a number of deals and discarding the face-up piles, you will be left with just three cards. You can then flip these over and show the spectators their cards.

Top tips

• Do not lose your concentration when you are performing this trick. Although each part of the trick is relatively easy, just one small mistake will ruin it.

• When dealing out the cards into face-up and face-down piles, always begin with a face-up card to guarantee success.

A family gathering

The magician deals out the four Jacks face up on the table. He then deals out the four Queens so that they are overlapping, then the Kings and finally the Aces. The four piles are collected together and dealt out again, this time face down. When the piles are turned over the cards have moved so that the four Jacks are now all together in one pile, as are the Queens, Kings and Aces. This is another great self-working trick.

Skill level ♦

How to do it

1 First you need to remove all the Jacks, Queens, Kings and Aces from the pack. Set aside the rest of the cards.

2 Deal out the four Jacks face up in a row on the table, alternating red and black. Next, deal the Queens on top of the Jacks, overlapping them so that the Jacks are still visible. Alternate these black, then red, and so on. Deal the four Kings on to these (red, black, red, black) and finally deal the Aces on top of the Kings (black, red, and so on).

3 Turn over each pile, squaring them up as you do, so the cards are now all face down. Gather up the piles so that the first pile is on top, followed by the second, third and then the fourth.

4 Now cut the cards two or three times or, if you prefer, you can ask a member of the audience to do this.

5 Square up the cards then, starting to the left, deal out four cards face down in a row. Deal the next four cards on top of these and so on, until all the cards have been used.

6 Now you can turn over each pile and fan out the cards so that the audience can see that all the Jacks are together in one pile, the Queens in another, the Kings in another and the Aces in another.

Text prediction

A spectator chooses a number between ten and 20 and the magician counts cards off the pack. He goes past the spectator's number, realizes his mistake and hands the pile over to the spectator to do it properly. The spectator counts off the number of cards and the magician asks her to turn the next card face up. Her phone then beeps with a new message – it is from the magician telling her the identity of the card! You will need to know the phone number of the volunteer for this trick, so it is not one you can perform randomly in front of anyone.

Skill level ♦♦

You will need
A mobile phone.

Preparation
Before you begin, memorize the seventh card in the pack and prepare a text message to the volunteer, stating the identity of that card. Shuffle the pack without disturbing the top seven cards (see page 12).

How to do it
1 Ask the volunteer to pick any number between ten and 20 and then begin counting off cards on to the table. Count in your head so it is not obvious when you have gone too far. Basically you need to count off seven cards more than her number.

2 Once you get there, pretend suddenly to realize that you have made a mistake, gather up the cards that you have dealt and put them back on top of the pack.

3 Hand the pack to the spectator and ask her to deal off the number of cards herself. While she is doing this hit 'send' on your phone so that the text message goes.

4 When she reaches the correct number of cards, tell her to deal the next card face up. Her phone should alert her to a new text message by then. Tell her to check it and it will be the prediction for the face-up card (below).

seven of clubs

Figure it out

Cards are dealt, divided and arranged according to their numbers. The magician is able to predict the number of a certain card on a certain pile. This is a really clever trick that requires some basic mental arithmetic and a bit of concentration. Easy to master yet it will not fail to impress!

Skill level ♦

How to do it

1 Shuffle the pack well, turn over the top card and lay it on the table, face up, to start your first pile. From now on Aces and picture cards have a value of one. You need to deal out cards on top of the first one to bring the number up to ten, using the value of the first card as your starting point. So, for example, if the first card is a Seven, you add three more cards; if it is a two, you add eight more, and so on. Deal the cards face up.

2 When you reach ten, start a new pile and continue making similar piles until you run out of cards. If you do not have enough cards left to complete a pile, keep these in your hand.

3 Looking at your piles, pick any three that have at least four cards in each. Turn these piles face down and collect all the other piles, adding them to the cards in your hand, if you have any.

4 Next, turn over the top card of any two of the face-down piles and add the numbers together. Take this number of cards from the stack in your hand and then take away another 19 cards. Count the remainder.

5 Turn over the top card of the last face-down stack. It will have the same value as the number of cards left in your hand!

Smooth calculator

A spectator removes a pile of cards from the pack and the magician is able to tell exactly how many cards have been removed. As long as you have got a reasonable head for numbers, this is a really easy trick that works every time.

Skill level ♦

How to do it

1 Shuffle the pack and ask for a volunteer from the audience. You can ask him if he would like to shuffle the pack as well. Ask him to take a small pile of cards from the top of the face-down pack and to put them behind his back so you cannot see them.

2 Now you also take a pile of cards from the pack. The important thing is to make sure you take a bigger pile than the spectator, otherwise the trick will fail.

3 Turn your back to the audience and ask the spectator to count the number of cards in his pile. Count your cards at the same time. Whatever your total is, minus three from it and tell the spectator that this is how many cards you have.

Top tip

The trick will only work if the spectator is holding fewer than fourteen cards and the magician is holding more cards than the spectator. To be on the safe side, always take a bigger pile than you think necessary – if you try to estimate by looking at the pile the spectator has taken, you might get it wrong.

4 Assuming your new total is 18 (21 with three deducted), turn back to face the spectator and tell him you have as many cards as he has, plus an extra three and as many extras that it might take to make his pile up to 18. Now ask for his total.

5 Assuming the spectator's total is 12, first deal out 12 cards. Now deal the extra three (but do not include these in your count) followed by your remaining cards, counting as you do so up to 18. This will work whatever the two totals are – as long as you remember to tell the spectator that you can make his pile up to whatever your new total is.

Cut to the chase

A spectator cuts the pack and chooses a card, which is cut back into the pack. The cards are then dealt into four piles. The magician eliminates cards and keeps dealing until there are just three cards remaining on the table. The magician picks out the spectator's card. This trick relies on the fact that the pack is split evenly into two piles – a couple of cards too many either way will ruin it.

Skill level ♦♦

How to do it

1 Shuffle the pack and place it on the table. Ask for a volunteer to cut the pack exactly in half. Make sure you are happy that the cut is even (below).

2 Ask the spectator to choose any card from either of the piles, memorize it and place it back on top of the pile she took it from. Next, ask her to place the other pile on top of that one, so the card is now lost in the pack.

3 The spectator must now deal the cards face down on to the table into four piles, going from left to right.

4 Turn over one pile at a time and spread out the cards so they are all visible. Ask the spectator to indicate whether the pile contains the card she chose. If it does, keep this pile and discard the others – if not, discard the pile and move on until you have the pile that does contain her chosen card.

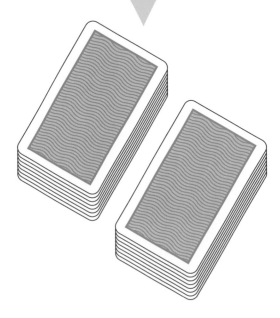

5 Square up the chosen pile, turn it face down and deal these cards into another four piles. There will be 13 cards to deal in total, so once the cards are dealt the first pile will have an uneven number of cards in it. Tell the spectator that you are going to remove that pile, as it is uneven compared to the other piles.

6 You are left with three piles of cards, each containing three cards. Ask the spectator to remove the top and bottom cards from each pile so that you are left with three cards on the table. Now ask her to discard the left and right cards, leaving just one in the middle. Ask what her chosen card was and turn over the remaining card – it is the one (below)!

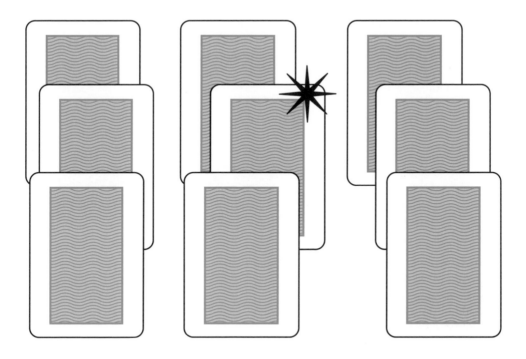

The incredible card scales

The magician holds the pack in one hand. A spectator makes a cut and places the cut pile in the magician's other hand. The magician then tells the spectator exactly how many cards are in the pile. This is another fantastic self-working trick that allows you to work out the number of cards in a pile. It will leave your audience truly baffled!

Skill level ♦♦♦

Preparation

First, you need to prepare the deck. Remove all the Spades and Hearts and arrange the Spades in order from the King at the top to the Ace at the bottom and arrange the Hearts in reverse. Now, starting with the King of Spades, pick up alternating cards from the two piles so that you end up with one pile that runs Spade, Heart, Spade, Heart, and so on. Split the remaining cards into two piles of 13 cards each and place one pile on top of the arranged cards and one underneath. Now turn the whole pack face down and you are ready to begin.

How to do it

1 Hold the pack in your left hand and ask a spectator to cut it wherever he likes, placing the cut section in your right hand. Move your hands around as if you are weighing up the cards. While you do this you need to glimpse the bottom card in your right hand.

2 If the bottom card is a Spade, you calculate the number of cards in your right hand. You do this by multiplying the value of the card by two and adding 13. So, for example, if the bottom card is the Five of Spades, you are holding 23 cards.

3 If the bottom card is a Heart the same principle applies for calculating the number of cards in your left hand but, in this instance you also need to subtract one from your total. So, for example, if the card is the Ten of Hearts this means you are holding 32 cards in your left hand.

Top tip

Apart from accuracy in your preparation, the key to this trick is to glimpse the bottom card without your audience noticing. Talk to the audience as you move your hands around, pretending to weigh the cards.

It's a kind of magic

The key to the tricks in this section lies in being able to provide a truly polished performance. Although a number of the tricks are quite simple, your success in convincing an audience will rely primarily on your ability to execute them quickly and smoothly. This means perfecting sleights such as palming, double lifting and false shuffling, but it also requires concentration and plenty of practice. Only then will you be able to perform with the slick dexterity that leaves an audience feeling they have witnessed real magic.

The twins

The magician gives a spectator two black Queens. He then begins dealing cards face down on to the table until the spectator tells him to stop. At that point the spectator places one of her twins on the pack. The process is repeated for the second Queen. At the end of the trick the magician fans through the pack to find that the two cards have located their siblings.

Skill level ◆

Preparation
Place one red Queen face down on top of the face-down pack and the other red Queen at the bottom of the pack. You also need to remove the two black Queens from the pack.

How to do it
1 Perform a false shuffle, keeping the top and bottom cards in place (see pages 9–10). Ask for a spectator and hand her the two black Queens, telling her that she is going to help you reunite them with their red twins.

2 Tell the spectator that you are going to begin dealing cards, face down, on to the table and she can tell you to stop whenever she likes. When she says 'Stop', instruct her to place one of the Queens face up on the dealt pile of cards. Place the remaining pack on top of this pile.

3 Repeat this process then square up the pack. Fan out the cards in front of the audience and ask the spectator to remove the face-up Queens and the cards directly to the right of them. On turning them over, she will discover that the red Queens have found their twins.

Top tip

This is a very easy trick to perform once the false shuffle has been mastered. However, it is important not to let the audience see that the bottom card is a red Queen or they will realize how the trick works.

Matching pairs

The magician selects two random cards from the pack and places them face down on the table. A spectator cuts the pack and the magician picks the top cards from each pile – they match the cards chosen at the beginning of the trick.

Skill level ♦♦

How to do it

1 Shuffle the pack of cards then fan through it, face up. Glimpse the top and bottom cards then pick out the two cards that match these. (So the Ten of Spades would be the match for the Ten of Clubs, and so on). It is important to remember which card is at the top and which is at the bottom.

2 Place the two chosen cards face down on the table. Perform a false shuffle with the rest of the pack so that the top and bottom cards stay in place (see pages 9–10).

3 Ask the spectator to cut the pack in two so that there are two piles of cards on the table. Turn over the top card of the top pile then turn over the matching card on the table (right).

4 Now flick over the other pile to reveal the bottom card. Turn over the remaining card on the table and you have two sets of pairs.

Top tip

Do not comment on why you turn the second pile over at the end – the audience will just assume that it is part of the trick and, once they see the matching card, it will not matter.

Five alive

The magician deals cards to four spectators who each have to pick and memorize one. After collecting the cards and dealing them out once more, the magician is able to pick out all the chosen cards. This is a great trick, involving a number of people, and it is almost impossible for anyone to work out how it is done.

Skill level ◆◆◆

How to do it

1 First, you need to make sure you have four willing audience members. It is best if all five of you are sitting down at a table.

2 You need to deal out five cards to each person, including yourself, dealing in rounds and beginning with the person to your left and finishing with yourself (below). When everyone has five cards each, you can set aside the remainder of the pack.

3 Ask the spectators to pick up their piles of cards and pick one card to memorize. They should not move the cards but simply square up their piles and place them back down on the table in front of them.

4 Now, again working from your left, gather up the piles of cards, putting each successive pile on top of the one before. Your pile needs to be the last one collected.

5 Deal out five rounds of cards once again. Take each pile in turn and fan the cards out in front of your spectators. Ask if anyone can see his card in the pile. The clever part of this trick is that, if someone does see his card, you can work out exactly which one it is from his position at the table. For example, if the person sitting three places from you says that his card is in the fan, you know that it is the third card in the fan (above).

Top tip

To add a little extra something to the trick, you could ask each spectator to write the identity of his chosen card on a piece of paper. Then, when it is time to reveal the cards, each could reveal his paper first and turn the card over next to it.

6 When someone says that he has seen his card, turn the cards to face you and remove the card, placing it face down in front of the spectator. Set aside the remainder of the pile and move on to the next one.

7 There might not be any chosen cards in a pile, in which case you simply set aside the whole pile. Equally, there could be more than one spectator's card in a pile. It will work in the same way and you just remove both cards, placing the correct one in front of each spectator.

8 Once everyone (apart from you) has a card in front of them, ask them all to turn their cards over and they will be amazed that they all have the card they chose at the beginning of the trick.

Pulled from the pack

A member of the audience is asked to select a card and memorize it. She then places it back in the pack wherever she likes. The magician throws the entire pack down on to the table but one card stays in his hand – the spectator's chosen card. You do not need any special skills to perform this trick but it does require a lot of practice to make it appear slick and convincing. Fast hands and dexterous fingers are essential!

Skill level ◆◆◆

How to do it

1 Shuffle the pack in front of the audience then fan out the pack and ask a member of the audience to pick any card, making sure you do not see it. Tell her to memorize the card.

2 While she is looking at the card very quickly and subtly turn over the bottom card so that it is face up and turn the pack over. You should now have a pack that is face up, apart from the top card, which is face down (below).

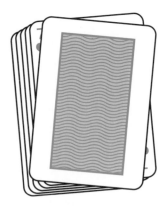

3 Hold the deck in your hand so that it is squared up and ask the spectator to insert her card anywhere in the pack.

4 Turn your back to the audience and explain that you are scanning the pack to divine which card the spectator chose. Keep talking as you do this.

5 Turn over the top card so that the whole pack should now be face up, apart from the card that the spectator chose. Locate the spectator's card and remove it from the pack. Turn the pack over and insert the spectator's card somewhere in the middle of the pack, face down, with the bottom edge sticking out about 1 cm (½ in) from the rest of the squared-up pack.

6 Turn back to the audience. Hold the pack by placing your little finger

solely on the spectator's card, your thumb on the card and the main pack and the rest of your fingers just on the pack (above). Throw the pack down on to the table, gripping the spectator's card so that it is left in your hand. You can then reveal it to your audience.

Top tips

- Try and make a comment while the spectator is looking at and memorizing her card to distract her attention away from what you are doing with the pack.

- When the spectator is inserting her chosen card back into the pack, be very careful not to let any of the cards slide around, otherwise she is going to see that the other cards are actually face up.

- Use your hand to try and cover the pack when you turn back to face the audience so they do not notice the bottom edge of the spectator's card sticking out.

Identity crisis

A card sits face up on top of the pack. The magician places a card face down on top of it then pulls it away again and the face-up card has changed identity. This is a very simple illusion that is often used to begin a routine and warm up the audience. It requires mastery of the double lift – and a steady hand!

Skill level ♦

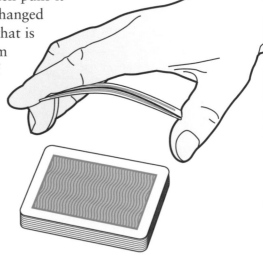

Preparation
Before performing the trick turn the second card in the pack face up (above).

How to do it
1 Shuffle the pack in front of the audience without disturbing the top two cards (see page 12).

2 You need to double lift the top two cards from the pack so that you end up holding the two cards that are face to face (see page 13 and above right). When you remove them, make sure that you point the two cards down and away from the audience so they cannot see the back of the face-up card.

3 With your other hand, turn over the new top card of the pack so that it is now face up and show your audience.

4 Now replace the top card(s), sliding them a little, as though you are trying to manipulate the face-up card. Release the concealed card discreetly as you do this. You can now remove the top card to reveal that the face-up card has switched identity.

Top tip

If you like, you could continue this trick by making the card switch back again. Simply put your card back on the pack, move it a little and perform the double lift to reveal the original face-up card once more.

Sit tight

A spectator chooses a card and returns it to the pack. The magician drops five cards to the floor and names one of them as the spectator's. However, this is not the spectator's card, and neither are the others. The magician looks confused but then sees that the spectator is sitting on a card – the one that he chose. This trick can only be performed in front of one spectator for obvious reasons! You will need to be quick and make sure you are sitting in a position that allows you to reach the spectator's chair without drawing attention to yourself.

Skill level ♦♦♦

How to do it

1 Shuffle the pack. Fan out the cards and ask the spectator to select one, memorize it and return it anywhere in the pack.

2 Create a break in the pack below the spectator's card. Pretend to square up the pack then cut it at the break, taking the top pile underneath so that the spectator's card is now on the bottom.

3 Tell the spectator that you will now pass him some of your magic to enable him to locate his chosen card in the pack. Fan out the cards, keeping the bottom card obscured, to prevent it from being chosen. Ask the spectator to select any five cards and hand them back to you. Keep the rest of the pack in your other hand.

4 Scatter the cards face down on the floor, making sure the cards are just beyond his reach so he has to lean forwards out of his chair in order to turn them over. Move towards the spectator as if you need to get a better look at the cards and point to one of them, claiming that this is his card. As he leans forwards to turn it over, drop his real card from the bottom of the pack on to his seat, face down.

5 When he turns the card on the floor over and says that it is not his, look confused and ask him to turn over the other cards to check those. You can move away again at this point.

6 When he has checked the other cards, look around on the floor and then look at his chair, telling him that he is sitting on a card. He will pick it up and be astonished to see that it is his chosen card.

Random selection

The magician riffles through the pack and a spectator says when to stop. At that point a card is removed and placed face down on the table. This is repeated three more times and when all the cards are turned over, they are the four Queens.

Skill level ♦♦

Preparation
Before you begin this trick, remove the four Queens from the pack and place them together at the bottom.

How to do it
1 Shuffle the pack in front of your audience, being careful not to move the bottom four cards (see page 12).

2 Ask for a volunteer and tell her that you are going to riffle through the pack slowly and she is to stop you whenever she likes. You will remove the card at the point where she says 'Stop'.

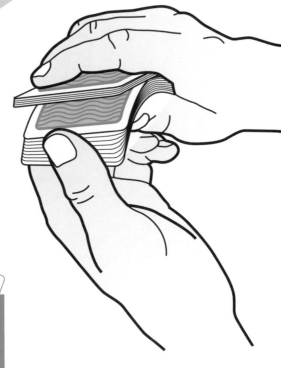

Top tip

The effectiveness of this trick depends entirely on the angle of the pack, so it is a good idea to practise it in front of a mirror. If you get the angle just right, it is a great illusion.

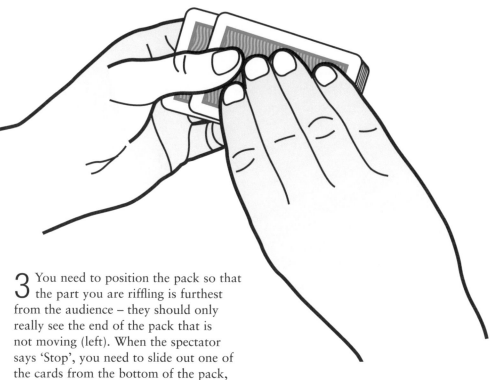

3 You need to position the pack so that the part you are riffling is furthest from the audience – they should only really see the end of the pack that is not moving (left). When the spectator says 'Stop', you need to slide out one of the cards from the bottom of the pack, bending it upwards as you do so, so that it appears to be coming from somewhere inside the pack (above). Place the card on the table.

4 This is repeated three more times until you have four cards face down and spread out on the table. Slowly turn each card over, revealing all four Queens.

Time on your hands

A spectator removes the cards from any suit of his choice from a pack of cards, except the King, and lays them out on the table in the form of a clock face. He then thinks of a time and removes that number of cards from the remaining pile, placing them on the bottom. He deals the whole pack randomly, face down, and the magician is able to point to the card that represents the suit and the time that the spectator chose. This is a fun trick to perform and the results are impressive. There is quite a lot to do so it is important that each stage is completed in the correct order and according to the instructions.

Skill level ♦♦

How to do it

1 Turn your back to the audience from the beginning of this trick and ask a volunteer from the audience to pick any suit he likes and remove all the cards of that suit from the deck, apart from the King. He can now shuffle the remaining pack, if he likes, and set it aside.

Top tip

As long as the spectator follows your instructions carefully, and you remember where the thirteenth card has been placed, you cannot fail with this trick. You can build up the excitement at the end of the trick by touching a few cards or letting both hands hover over the table for a few moments before going to the chosen card.

2 Tell him to arrange the cards face up on the table to represent a clock face, beginning with the Ace at one o'clock, all the way round to the queen at midday (top right). He must now look at the clock face and concentrate hard on a specific hour – this will give him the card that you are going to try and locate, for example the Four of Hearts.

3 Still with your back turned to the audience, ask the spectator to collect together the clock cards in their numerical order and place them on top of the remaining pack, face down and one at a time, starting with the Ace.

4 He must think of the hour or number he chose and take this number of cards from the bottom of the pack, moving them, one by one to the top of the pack.

5 Now you can turn round. Ask the spectator to deal the whole pack, face down, on to the table in a completely random order. The key now is to concentrate on the thirteenth card to be laid. Memorize exactly where this is placed – this is the only thing you need to concentrate on.

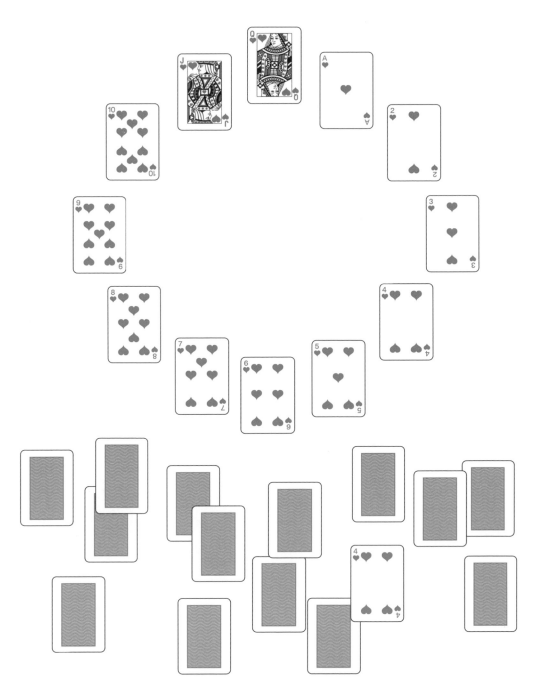

6 At this point you can use any dialogue or actions that you like to add some suspense to the trick. Go to the correct card immediately or waver over a couple of others first, trying to pick up the 'vibe' of the chosen card. When you eventually turn over the card it will be the suit that the spectator chose and the hour that he picked from the clock face (above).

Pick of the bunch

A pack of playing cards is spread out, face down, over the table. A member of the audience is asked to attempt to locate two specific cards and then the magician locates another. When the magician reveals the cards to the audience they are indeed the exact ones that were asked for. There are not so many card skills involved here as a good memory and a calm approach.

Skill level ♦♦

How to do it

1 Shuffle a pack of cards in front of the audience, taking a subtle peak at the card at the bottom of the pack.

2 Randomly spread all the cards out face down on the table, memorizing where the bottom card ends up.

3 Ask for a volunteer from the audience and tell her that you are going to ask her to guess the location of two specific cards. Call out the name of the card you have memorized and tell the spectator to point to the card she thinks it is. Pick up the card she has pointed to but do not show it to her.

4 You now call out the name of the card you have just picked up and ask her to point to the card on the table that she thinks it is. Once again you pick up the card she has chosen, without revealing it.

5 You then say you are going to give it a try. Call out the name of the card you have just picked up, hover your hand over the cards on the table as if you are deep in thought, and eventually go for the card that was originally at the bottom of the pack.

6 You can now reveal the three cards to the audience and they will be the three that you have called out (below).

- If you want to perform the trick with more than three cards, you can keep going for as many as you like. Just make sure that you always pick up the bottom card last of all.

- When calling out the names of the cards to be picked, try to make it look as random as possible so that no one works out the link between the cards you are holding and the next card to be called.

Variation

Instead of spreading the cards out on the table, keep them squared up. Again you need to memorize the bottom card then perform a false shuffle so your audience does not suspect anything (see page 10). Assume the bottom card was the **Queen of Hearts**. Ask a spectator to remove the top card from the pile and place it on the table. Tell the audience that this card is the Queen of Hearts then look at the card but do not show the audience. Announce that you were correct and keep hold of the card (say the **Nine of Spades**). Now ask the spectator to pick a card from anywhere in the middle of the pack and again place it on the table. Tell them you think this is the Nine of Spades and again look at the card, hold on to it and tell them you were right (say the **Ace of Hearts**). Ask the

spectator to do the same with the bottom card of the pack and announce it is the Ace of Hearts. Of course this card is actually the Queen of Hearts although you announce that it is the Ace of Hearts. Now you have all three correct cards and you can reveal them to your amazed audience (below).

The Kings return home

The magician removes the four Kings from the pack and tells the audience that three of them are being sent on an urgent mission. The pack is dealt into piles with the Kings lost among them. The cards are dealt out again, and the piles are removed until there are only three cards left – they are the three Kings returning home. This trick is a real test of memory and it is important to get each step exactly right. The trick itself is easy but will take a few rehearsals to learn properly.

Skill level ♦♦♦

Preparation
Remove all the Kings from the pack and place them face up on the table (below).

How to do it

1 Shuffle the pack well in front of the audience then deal out a pile of 14 cards and two piles of 15 cards in a row on the table. You will be left with four cards, which you place in another pile at the end of the first three.

2 Ask for a volunteer and tell him to shuffle each pile of cards in turn, as thoroughly as he wishes, returning them to the same place.

3 Now the spectator needs to place one of the Kings face down on top of the first pile. He can then take as many cards as he likes from the second pile and place these on top of the first pile. Then he puts the next King face down on the second pile, takes as many cards as he likes from the third pile and places these face down on the second pile. He places a third King face down on the third pile of cards and the fourth pile is placed face down on top of that. The fourth King must stay at home to guard the castle from invaders.

4 Tell the spectator to pick up the first pile then place the second pile on top and the third pile on top of that.

5 Take the cards from the spectator and, starting from the left, begin dealing off cards, face down, alternately into two piles. Continue until all the cards have been used.

6 Now take the first pile of cards and deal the first card face down on to the second pile. The next card is dealt on to the table to begin another pile, and so on, until the cards have all been used.

7 Pick up the smallest pile and repeat the process once more – so the first card goes on to the big pile, the next starts a new pile. You need to keep doing this dealing until there are just three cards left.

8 Set aside the big pile and place the three face-down cards next to the remaining face-up King. Tell the audience that the mission has been a success and the other Kings are now returning home. Turn over the three cards and reveal the three Kings.

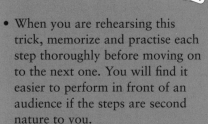

Top tips

- When you are rehearsing this trick, memorize and practise each step thoroughly before moving on to the next one. You will find it easier to perform in front of an audience if the steps are second nature to you.

- The spectator needs to understand your instructions for the trick to work successfully so make sure you make them as clear as possible to avoid confusion.

Lucky Sevens

A spectator cuts a shuffled pack into four separate piles. The magician asks her to move some cards around to different piles and when she has finished, the magician asks her to turn over the top card of each pile – they are all Sevens. This is a really quick trick to learn, which makes it a great introduction to a routine.

Skill level ♦

Preparation
Before you begin this trick, locate the four Sevens and put them face down on top of the face-down pack.

How to do it
1 Perform a false shuffle, keeping the top four cards in place (see page 12), then square up the pack and ask for a volunteer from the audience.

2 Hand the pack to the spectator and ask her to cut the pack into four roughly equal piles and line them up on the table (below). Make sure you note which pile has the Sevens on top of it. Hopefully it will be the first or last, as this will make the trick flow better, but it does not really matter.

3 Ask the spectator to work her way along the piles, directing her to the pile with the Sevens on top last. She needs to pick up each pile and move the top three cards to the bottom of the pile. She then needs to deal one card on top of the other three piles and place the pile back on the table.

4 When she has finished, the top card of each pile will now be a Seven. Tell the audience that the lucky Sevens always find some way of reaching the top. Ask the spectator to turn the top card over on each pile and sure enough, the Sevens have made it.

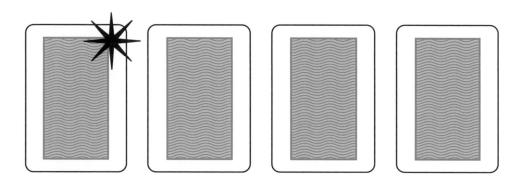

Be prepared

Even the most successful magicians cannot rely on their beguiling personas and sleights of hand alone for a truly outstanding performance. Indeed, a good number of the most impressive card tricks require at least some preparation in advance. This selection of tricks illustrates a number of classic examples as to how a pack of cards can be doctored slightly – either by marking, bending or cutting cards, or by arranging the cards in a very specific way – and this can be all it takes to perform show-stopping magic of the very highest quality.

The marked card

A spectator is asked to name any card in the deck. The magician then fans through the deck, finds the spectator's card and pulls it out to reveal that it has been marked with an 'X'. It is best to use an old pack of cards for this trick, or to make sure that you want to perform the trick often, as you will not be able to use the pack for other tricks afterwards.

Skill level ◆◆◆

You will need
A Joker.

Preparation
Before you begin the trick, you need to divide the pack exactly in two (it does not matter which cards go in which pile, as long as there are 26 cards in each). Using a marker pen, write the letter 'X' on the front, and towards the left, of each card in one pile and on the back, and towards the right, of each card in the other pile (below). The position of the mark is important, as it will minimize the risk of the audience spotting an 'X' on any of the cards. Turn both piles of cards face down, place a Joker face down on the pile with the marks on the back and put the other pile on top of it.

 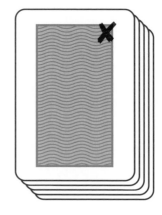

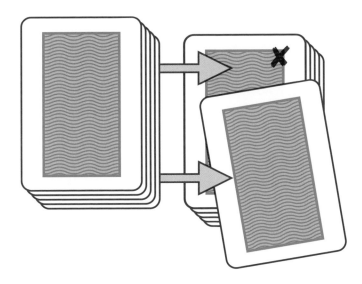

How to do it

1 Ask for a volunteer to name any card in the deck. Carefully fan out the pack towards you, revealing as little as possible of each card in order to keep the 'X's hidden.

2 Locate the spectator's card and, if it has the 'X' on the back, slide it from the pack and place it face up on the table. If the 'X' is on the front, place the card face down on the table. (To make it easy, cards to the left of the Joker will have an 'X' on the front and those to the right will have it on the back.)

3 Making sure that none of the 'X's on the other cards are visible, carefully place the fanned-out pack on the table behind the spectator's card. This is so that the audience can see there are not any marks on the other cards.

4 Tell the audience that, before you began the trick, you marked one card with an 'X'. Turn over the spectator's card and they will see that this is the marked card.

The gossiping sisters

A spectator places three Queens throughout a pack of cards but, with one simple cut of the deck, they magically appear together again.

Skill level ♦

Preparation
Before you begin the trick, place one of the Queens face down on top of a face down pack of cards.

How to do it
1 Fan through the pack of cards in front of the audience, picking out the remaining three Queens. Do not let the audience see the one you have placed. Ask for a volunteer and hand the three Queens to her.

2 Perform a false shuffle, moving the fourth queen to the bottom of the pack (see page 11). Square up the pack, place it on the table in front of you and tell the audience that the three sisters have been gossiping so much that you want to split them up. Ask the spectator to place one Queen on top of the pack, one on the bottom and one somewhere in the middle.

3 Now ask the spectator to cut the pack anywhere she likes, moving the top section of the cut to the bottom of the pack.

4 Lift the pack to your ear and tell the audience you think you can hear the sisters gossiping again so you are going to make sure they are still apart in the pack. Fan through the cards in front of the audience and to everyone's surprise, the gossiping sisters are back together in the middle of the pack (below)!

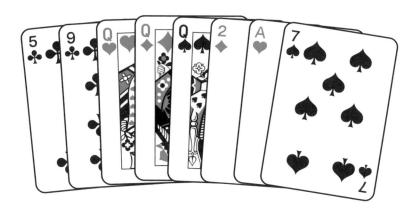

A colourful calling

The pack is shuffled and the cards fanned out face down on the table. As if by magic the magician is able to pick cards randomly and guess the colour of each correctly.

Skill level ◆◆

Preparation
Before you begin, separate the red and black cards into two piles (below).

With the black pile face down in your hands bend the whole pile away from you, creating a very slight curve. Do the opposite with the red pile – that is, with the pile face down bend the cards towards you (below). Put the piles back together and you are ready to begin.

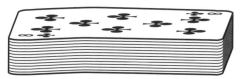

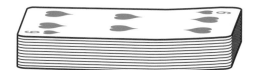

Top tips

- Be extremely careful not to bend the cards too much, as this will give the game away.

- To draw out the effect of your 'divining' powers, why not hover your hands over the cards or lean back with your eyes shut as you call out each colour?

How to do it
1 Shuffle the pack of cards in front of your audience then spread them out on the table in front of you. You should easily be able to tell the red cards from black by the way each bends but, because the effect is so slight, your audience will not notice a thing.

Aces on the case

The four Aces sit on the table, ready to delve into the pack and rescue a kidnapped card. A spectator chooses a card, memorizes it and then replaces it on top of the pack. This is the kidnapped card. The pack is cut and the card is lost so the Aces are inserted to try and find it. The magician leaves the Aces protruding from the pack, taps the pack, end-on, on the table and the three kidnappers pop out the other end. The magician says that the Ace detectives are obviously on the right track. The pack is tapped on the table again and two of the Aces are visible. The magician taps the pack once more and the spectator's kidnapped card pops out – the Aces have rescued it.

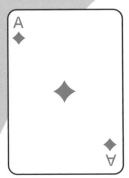

Skill level ♦♦♦♦

Preparation
Before you begin, remove the four Aces from the pack and place them face up in a row on the table (above).

How to do it
1 Shuffle the pack in front of the audience, glimpsing the bottom card as you do. Ask for a volunteer and tell him that he is going to help in a kidnap case. The Ace detectives have been alerted that a kidnap attempt is about to take place.

2 Fan out the cards and ask the spectator to select one and memorize it. Square up the pack and tell the spectator to return his card on the top. This is the kidnap victim. The spectator can then cut the pack, moving the top section under the bottom, and you can tell him that the kidnappers have now got away with their victim and the Ace detectives will try to solve the case.

3 Fan through the deck of cards until you find the bottom card that you glimpsed – the card to the right of this will be the spectator's. Tell the audience that you are inserting the Aces to try and track down the kidnappers and rescue the victim. Place one Ace before the bottom card that you glimpsed and one after it. Place another after the spectator's card and the final one after the card following that. The order should be as follows: Ace, bottom card, Ace, spectator's card, Ace, random card, Ace (above). The Aces should only be inserted halfway into the pack.

4 Square up the pack – the four Aces should be sticking out at the top. Now, holding the pack by its sides with your thumb on one side and your fingers on the other, turn it upside down and firmly tap the Aces against the table. They should slide in and three cards should slide out at the opposite end – the cards between the Aces. Do not let the audience see these cards but tell them that they are the three kidnappers and that the Aces are close on their tail.

5 Repeat this process, hitting the protruding cards on the table. This time two of the Aces should pop out at the opposite end of the pack. Tell the audience that the Aces have split up and that these two are closing in on the kidnappers. You can let the audience see the cards this time.

6 Finally, hit the cards on the table once more and, this time, the spectator's card should come out on its own (left). Tell the audience that the Aces have been successful and have rescued the kidnapped card.

A good guess

The magician deals ten cards from a shuffled pack. He fans them out on the table and the spectator picks one. The magician is able to name the spectator's card.

Skill level ♦

Preparation
Before you begin, remove the ten cards running from the Ace of Hearts to the Ten of Hearts from the pack. Arrange the cards, face up, so that the Ace is at the bottom of the pile and the Ten is at the top (right). Square up the pile, turn it face down and put it on top of the pack.

How to do it

1 Perform a false shuffle in front of the audience, keeping these top ten cards in place (see page 12).

2 Deal ten cards on to the table, and set aside the rest of the pack. Gather up the cards and fan them out face down. From your perspective the cards will be running from the Ace on the left to the Ten on the right.

3 Ask a volunteer to pick and remove any card. You can work out which card she has taken by counting in from the left. So, for example, if hers is the fourth card, you know it is the Four of Hearts (below).

4 You can now reveal the identity of the spectator's card to your amazed audience.

Stacks of royalty

A spectator shuffles the pack and deals out four piles of cards. On turning over the top card of every pile, a Queen is revealed. Furthermore, when the second card on every pile is turned over, they are all Kings. This is an easy trick that will impress your audience but should not be repeated on the same people, as they will probably have worked it out by the second or third demonstration.

Skill level ♦

Preparation

Remove all the Kings and Queens from the pack. Place the four Kings face down on top of the face-down pack, followed by the four Queens.

How to do it

1 Shuffle the pack in front of your audience. You will need to perform a false shuffle here, as you do not want to disturb the top eight cards – they must stay at the top in the correct order (see page 12).

2 Ask for a volunteer from the audience, give her the cards and tell her to deal out about half the pack, alternately, into two piles. Set aside the rest of the pack.

3 Now ask her to deal each of the two piles into two piles of cards. There should now be four small piles of cards on the table.

Top tip

The false shuffle is the key to this trick, as you have to convince your audience that the pack has been thoroughly shuffled. It is also very important that the spectator deals out the cards alternately when making the different piles.

4 Ask the spectator to remove and turn over the top card from each pile – they will be the four Queens. You can then say something like 'Where there is a Queen, there is also usually a King'. Now ask the spectator to remove and turn over the next card on the top of each pile and, sure enough, they will be the four Kings.

Suited and booted

A spectator chooses any card they like from the pack. The pack is then cut, first by the magician and then by the spectator. When the spectator makes his cut, the magician counts off cards corresponding to the face value of the card that was cut to. On turning over the last card, it is revealed as the one the spectator chose at the beginning of the trick.

Skill level ♦♦

Preparation
Before you begin the trick, remove all of the cards of one suit from Ace to Ten. Arrange the cards in numerical order with the Ace at the top, and place them face down at the bottom of the face-down pack – the Ace should be the very last card.

How to do it
1 Perform a false shuffle so that the arranged cards on the bottom of the pack do not change position or order (see page 12).

2 Ask for a volunteer from the audience, fan the cards out in your hand and ask the spectator to choose any card and remove it from the pack. You will need to keep the arranged cards at the bottom of the pack bunched up together and out of view in the pack, to avoid the spectator choosing one of these (below).

3 Square up the pack of cards and ask the spectator to memorize his chosen card and then place it back on top of the pack. Cut the pack so that the arranged suit is now on top of the spectator's chosen card.

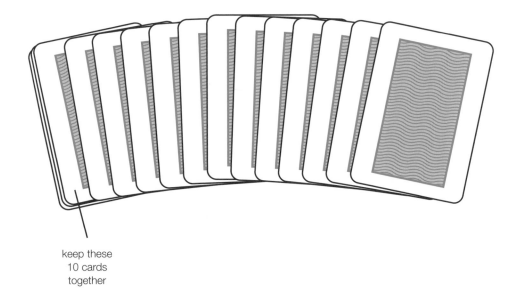

keep these
10 cards
together

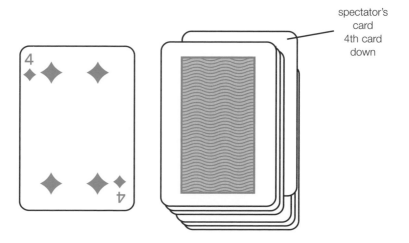

spectator's
card
4th card
down

4 Hand the cards to the spectator and ask him to turn the pack face up and make a cut wherever he likes. The idea is for him to reveal one of the cards from your arranged suit – this needs to happen in order for the trick to work. If he cuts to a card from your suit first time, great. If not, do not worry. Simply ask him to cut the pack again. He will not get suspicious if you say it naturally; he will just assume that a number of cuts are required to perform the trick. If the cut is not made at your suit, the spectator should finish the cut by putting the cut section underneath the pack before cutting again.

5 Once the spectator has cut to a card in your arranged suit, ask him to leave both sections of the pack on the table without completing the cut – with the bottom section face up and the top section face down (above). Pick up the face-down section and count off the number of cards that corresponds to the top card of the face-up pile. When you reach the last number, turn over the card to reveal it as the spectator's.

King of the castle

A pack of cards is riffled through, face down, on four separate occasions. Each time a member of the audience indicates for the magician to stop. The pack is then cut at that point and the next card is removed and placed on the table in front of the audience. When there are four cards laying face down they are turned over, revealing the four Kings. This trick can be perfected with just a little practice and is very convincing.

Skill level ◆◆

Preparation

Before you begin, go through the pack of cards removing all four Kings, plus any other two cards of your choice. Place the Kings face up on the table in two piles and put one of the other cards, face up, on top of each pile. Now place one pile face down on top of the other, face-up, pile (below). Finally, with the remainder of the pack face down on the table, place this pile of cards on top.

How to do it

1 Ask a member of the audience to help with the trick and tell her that you are going to riffle through the pack and she must say 'Stop' at any point. Now riffle though the pack, making sure you begin below the top six cards, as these must not be moved or separated.

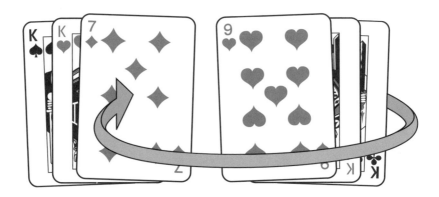

2 When you are told to stop, split the pack at that point and turn over the riffled section of cards so that they are face up at the top of the squared up pack. Slowly fan out the deck in front of the audience and, when you get to the first face-down card, place it on the table in front of you, face down. This will be a King rather than the real 'next' card at the split. Be very careful not to reveal the other hidden face-up cards that follow. Now place the riffled section of cards at the bottom of the pack, facing down.

3 Repeat this process three more times, with a different spectator stopping you each time, until there are four cards face down on the table. Now you can turn these cards over to reveal the four Kings (below). It works every time!

Top tip

Be very careful not to reveal any of the face-up cards in the pack as you riffle through – the slightest evidence of these will ruin the trick. Fan through the cards one at a time as you look for the first face-down card.

Match from the pack

A spectator chooses one of two decks and the cards are gradually eliminated by cutting and choosing piles. Eventually there is only one card left, and when the magician turns over the top or bottom card of the other pack, they match! This trick is easy to practise on your own and it is worth spending the time doing so in order to appear slick and fast when you perform it.

Skill level ◆◆◆

You will need
A second identical pack of cards.

Preparation
Before you begin you need to prepare the packs by choosing any two cards and placing them at the top and bottom of each pack. Memorize the cards and their positions. You should now have two packs with identical cards at the top and bottom (below).

How to do it

1 Ask for a volunteer from the audience to choose one of the packs of playing cards and then put the other to one side.

2 Now ask the spectator to cut the pack and place the two piles on the table. Ask him to select one of the piles and put the other to one side. Make sure you remember whether the selected pile contains the memorized card at the top or bottom.

3 Ask him to further cut his selected pile into two, again placing both piles on the table. This time you choose the pile to keep and you have to select the pile that contains your memorized card. Set aside the other pile.

4 Tell the spectator to pick up the selected pile and deal it as evenly as possible into four separate piles of cards. Concentrate here, as you need to know which pile your memorized card finishes in. When he has dealt out all the cards, ask him to select any two piles so you can eliminate one – pick one that does not contain your memorized card and set it to one side.

5 Now point to the two piles that do not contain your card and ask the spectator to choose one to eliminate. Remove the chosen pile and combine the last two piles, being careful to make sure that your memorized card ends up on either the very top or the very bottom of the new pile.

6 Pass the cards to the spectator and ask him to deal them out as evenly as possible into three piles. Indicate the two piles that do not contain your memorized card and ask him to choose one of these to eliminate. Put them to one side and combine the remaining two piles, again making sure that your card is either on the top or bottom of the pile.

7 There should be just a few cards left at this stage. If the number is odd and your card is at the bottom of the pile, simply deal the cards face down into two piles, turning over the last one, which will be your original card. If the number is odd and your card is at the top of the pile, ask the spectator to deal and eliminate the last card so the piles are the same. Continue asking the spectator to pick a pile and either keep or eliminate it, depending on whether it contains your card. Keep going until there are just two cards remaining. This time you choose which to eliminate then turn over the remaining card, which will be the one you memorized at the beginning of the trick.

8 If there is an even number of cards left again you simply keep dealing and eliminating as above.

9 Once you are left with just one playing card on the table, move the other pack to the centre of the table and, remembering which card was on top of the pack and which was on the bottom, you pull off that card to match the one left on the table.

Top tip

To make the trick even more convincing, you might choose to shuffle both the packs of cards in front of the audience before you begin the trick. You will need to perform a false shuffle here, as the top and bottom cards from each pack must not be disturbed.

Take it from the top

The magician gives a member of the audience two cards – a black Eight and a black Nine – and asks her to return them anywhere in the pack. Without shuffling or disturbing the pack in any way, the magician then holds it face down in front of the audience, taps it twice and peels off the top two cards, which are the ones that were just replaced.

Skill level ◆

Preparation
Before you begin the trick, place the Eight of Clubs and the Nine of Spades face down on top of the pack (below).

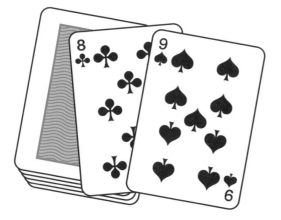

How to do it
1 Remove the Eight of Spades and the Nine of Clubs from the pack and give these to a member of the audience (below). Ask the spectator to replace these cards anywhere in the pack.

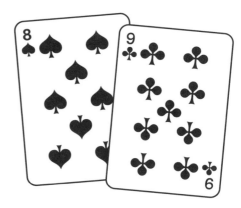

2 Hold the pack of cards in front of you in one hand, face down, and tap it twice firmly with your other hand. Wait a couple of seconds for effect before slowly peeling off the top two cards and laying them on the table in front of the audience. The cards will be the Eight of Clubs and Nine of Spades but your audience will think they are the same cards they were handed earlier (above).

Top tip

Don't mention the suits of the initial two cards at all during the trick as you do not want to alert your audience to the fact that the cards at the end are different from those removed from the pack at the beginning.

Double decker

A pack is split into two and a spectator is asked to choose and memorize one card from each pile. Simply by shuffling through the two piles, the magician can pull out the spectator's chosen cards.

Skill level ♦

Preparation

Before you begin the trick separate the pack into two piles, according to colour. Square up the two piles and set them both face down on the table.

How to do it

1 Ask for a volunteer and tell her she can choose any one card from each of the piles. Fan out the first pile, face down, in front of the spectator so she can remove a card and memorize it. Square up the pile, put it back on the table and tell the spectator to lay her card face down in front of the pile. Now do the same with the other pile.

Top tip

You might want to allow the spectator to shuffle the piles of cards after returning her chosen cards. However, there is a danger that she will see the cards face up and work out what is going on. Generally, if you shuffle the cards, she will not suspect anything and will still think that the shuffle has mixed up the cards.

2 When both cards have been chosen and placed on the table, switch over the piles and tell the spectator to return the cards to anywhere in the, now different, piles. Basically she is replacing the red card to a pile of black cards and vice versa.

3 Shuffle each of the piles thoroughly and return them to the table. Taking one pile, fan out the cards facing you and simply pull out the only card that is a different colour to the rest (above). Lay it face down in front of the spectator and repeat the process with the other pile of cards. Now you can turn the cards over to reveal that they are the ones chosen by the spectator.

The four conspirators

A spectator chooses a card, which is put to one side. The magician performs a number of different cuts and eliminations with the remainder of the pack and ends up with the three remaining cards of the same rank.

Skill level ♦♦

Preparation

Before you begin this trick you need to go through the pack and remove any two complete sets of four cards. So, for example, take out all the Tens and Queens. Arrange the pack so that one set appears on top of the other at the top of the face-down pack. For this example, place the Tens on top of the pack, followed by the Queens.

How to do it

1 If you are confident with false shuffles, shuffle the pack in front of the audience, being careful not to disturb the top eight cards (see page 12).

2 Deal the top eight cards face down on to the table in two parallel rows of four, each row containing the set of four arranged cards – so the Tens would be in a row at the top and the Queens would be in a row underneath.

3 Ask for a volunteer and tell him to choose a row to be eliminated. It does not matter which he chooses at this stage. Assume that the Tens are picked. Collect the cards in that row and place them on the bottom of the pack.

4 Now ask the spectator to choose any card in the remaining row – he should not turn it over, he just needs to indicate it as his chosen card. Put this card face down in the centre of the table and gather up the other three cards, placing them on top of the pack. These will be the three Queens.

5 Now ask the spectator to cut the pack and discard the bottom section (you want to keep the pile with the three Queens on top).

6 Deal this pile into three smaller piles in a row behind the spectator's chosen card, so the bottom card of each will be a Queen. Tell the spectator that he can now turn over the card he chose.

7 Remind the audience of the name of the trick and slowly turn over each of the three piles to reveal the fellow conspirators (below).

Runaway Jacks

The Jacks have run away and the audience has to help the magician find them. After the magician shuffles the deck, a spectator chooses a number. That many cards are removed and the first Jack is located. This is repeated until all the Jacks have been found safe and sound. You will need to keep your concentration for this trick and have perfected the art of the false shuffle. You will also need to have an audience of at least four people, as four volunteers are required to locate the Jacks.

Skill level ♦♦

Preparation

Before you begin, prepare the pack by removing all four Jacks. You also need to remove a set of cards from any suit, ranging from Two to Nine inclusive. Place them in their correct numerical order and square them up. Place the pack face down on the table and put the four Jacks on top, followed by the set of eight cards. You should now have a pack with the first 12 cards as follows: Two, Three, Four, Five, Six, Seven, Eight, Nine, Jack, Jack, Jack, Jack.

How to do it

1 Ask for a volunteer from the audience, saying you need help to locate the four Jacks, who have run away. Shuffle the pack in front of the audience, making sure that you do not disturb the top twelve cards (see page 12).

2 Ask the spectator to pick a number between ten and 19 and count off that number of cards, face down on the table. Place the pack down and square up the pile of counted cards.

3 Next, ask the spectator to add together the two digits of her chosen number to give one single digit. (For example, if her original number was 14, she will end up with five.) Pick up the pile of counted-off cards and count the new number of cards back on to the remaining pack. Peel off the next card from the pile and place it on the table face up – this will be the first runaway Jack!

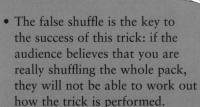

4 Put the pile of counted-off cards back on top of the rest of the pack and shuffle the cards, again being careful not to disturb the top 11 (one has now been removed).

5 Repeat the process three more times, with three different volunteers, until all the Jacks have been found (below).

Top tips

- The false shuffle is the key to the success of this trick: if the audience believes that you are really shuffling the whole pack, they will not be able to work out how the trick is performed.

- Keep up a good pace so that the audience stays interested and confused throughout the whole of your performance.

Red eye

In this simple but effective card trick using two different packs of cards, the magician predicts the colour of the card that a spectator will choose from a selection of ten.

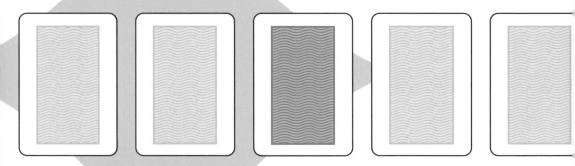

Skill level ♦♦

You will need

A pen and paper. An extra pack of cards with a different design on the back.

Preparation

Before you begin the trick, write 'I predict that the card you choose will be red' on a piece of paper. Fold the paper up and put it in your pocket. Prepare the cards for the trick by taking two packs with different designs on the back of the cards – one pack must have a red design. Lay the packs out on the table and take any black card from the pack with the red design. Set aside the remainder of this pack. Now take any eight black cards of your choice and one red card of your choice from the other pack and set aside the rest of the pack. You should

now be holding ten playing cards. Arrange the cards in a pile with a face-up card on top, then a face-down card and so on. You need to make sure that the third card is the card with the red design (this will be face up, hiding the design) and the fourth card is the red-faced card (this will be face down, hiding the red face). This should all be done before you start the trick (below).

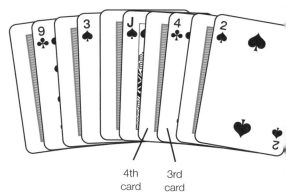

4th card   3rd card

 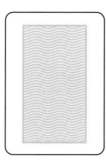 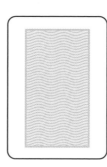 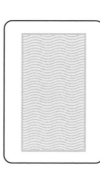 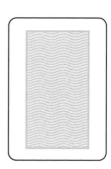

How to do it

1 Ask for a volunteer to help you from the audience. Deal the ten cards out on the table in front of them, moving from left to right. Ask him to pick a number between one and ten.

2 Now comes the tricky part that calls for some memory powers:

- If the spectator chooses seven or eight, you count in from right to left.

- If he chooses three or four, you count in from left to right.

- If he chooses any other number (one, two, five, six, nine or ten), begin at the left and spell out that number, tapping each card in the line as you say each letter.

3 Whichever number the spectator chooses, you will finish at the third or fourth card from the left of the line. If you land on the third card, turn all the other face-up cards over, leaving the third card until last. When you turn this over, it will have a red design – the only one like this in the line (above).

4 If you land on the fourth card, turn all the face-down cards face up, finishing with the fourth card, which will be the only red-faced card in the line-up.

5 Now you can say something like 'I knew you would pick a red card. In fact, I was so convinced that I wrote it down earlier.' Go to your pocket and remove the piece of paper with your prediction on and show the audience to finish the trick.

The literate magician

The deck is shuffled and the top 13 cards are counted off. With the cards face down the magician begins to spell out each card name in turn, starting with the ace (so 'A', 'C' then 'E'). The card following the final letter is always that which has just been spelt! When you reach the King, you will have all 13 cards on the table in the correct order.

Skill level ♦♦

Preparation

Before you begin, remove a set of 13 cards from the deck from Ace through to King. Pick cards of different suits to help with the illusion later on. Now place the cards in the following order – it is essential to get this right for the trick to work. Put the Three on the table, face up, then on top of that place the remaining cards as follows: Eight, Seven, Ace, Queen, Six, Four, Two, Jack, King, Ten, Nine and lastly, Five. Put these cards back on top of the deck, face down (below).

Top tip

Spell out the cards slowly and carefully – one small slip could ruin the entire trick.

How to do it

1 Shuffle the cards, making sure you do not disturb the top 13 or place any other cards on top of them (see page 12). As the top cards do not look like a set, you can freely show the audience the deck to prove there is nothing unusual about the pack.

2 Next, remove the top 13 cards (the prepared set) and discard the rest of the pack. Keep the cards face down and, starting with Ace, call out 'A' removing the top card to the bottom of the pile, and then do the same with 'C' and 'E'. Turn over the next card on the pile to reveal an Ace. Show it to the audience and place it, face up, on the table in front of them. Continue with Two, Three, and so on, placing each card on the table to build up eventually to the complete set of 13.

Jumping through hoops

The magician claims to be able to walk through a playing card. To the amusement and astonishment of the audience he proceeds to do so. This is a fun trick that is ideal for parties. It is all down to the preparation so that you can perform the trick at a moment's notice.

Skill level ♦♦♦

You will need
A craft knife. A ruler. A cutting board.

Preparation
Before you start the trick you will need to spend some time preparing the pack and one card in particular. This card will be ruined, so either use an old pack of cards or take a card from a pack in which other cards are already missing or damaged.

Place the card on a cutting board. Using a small, sharp craft knife, carefully cut through the card, down its middle (below left). Do not cut right to the edges of the card, which would cut it in two, but leave about 0.5 cm (¼ in) at either end. Fold the card along the cut and make a series of cuts across the width of the card, at right angles to the first cut. The first should run from the cut itself almost to the outer edge of the card. The next should run from the outer edge, stopping short of the main cut and so on, until you have a series of cuts all the way down the card (below right). You will need a good number of these cuts for the trick to work, so keep them close together. Now smooth the card flat and place it somewhere in the middle of the pack.

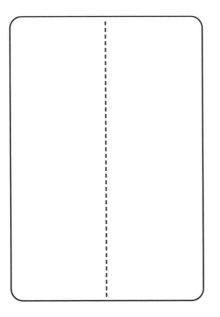

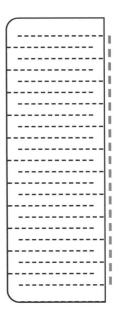

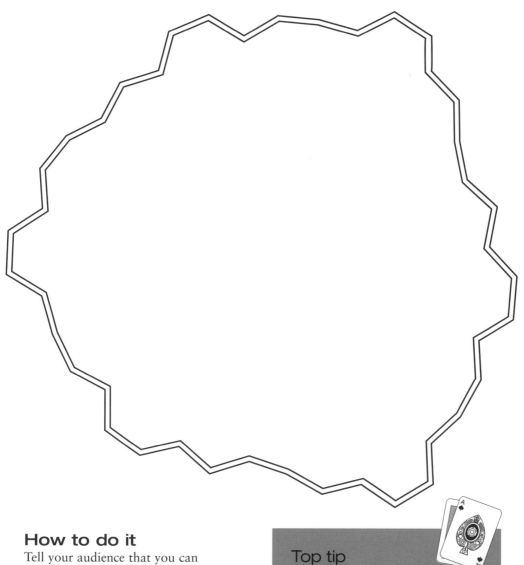

How to do it

Tell your audience that you can physically walk through a playing card and offer to prove it. When the audience responds, casually fan through the pack until you reach the prepared card, carefully open it up to form a big hoop that you can then walk through (above).

Top tip

You can either perform this trick as part of a show, or you can casually wander up to a group of people at a party, announcing that you can walk through a playing card. Keep your cool and be very careful not to tear the card before you have walked through it.

Mixing then matching

A spectator selects two cards from the pack and replaces them randomly. The magician then flips through the pack, removing two face-up cards along with the face-down cards that are next to them. When the face-down cards are turned over by the spectator, they are revealed to be partners of the face-up cards.

Skill level ♦♦♦♦

Preparation

Before you begin the trick, you need to arrange the pack so that the cards run in pairs, according to their value and colour. So, the cards should go black Aces, red Aces, black Twos, red Twos, black Threes, red Threes and so on right through to Kings (right). Turn the pack face down.

How to do it

1 Ask for a volunteer to choose a card from the fanned out pack, pulling it slightly out of the deck to indicate her choice. Make a cut in the pack above the chosen card and place the cut cards under the rest of the pack. Now the spectator can turn over her card so that it is face up on the face-down pack.

2 Make a cut roughly halfway through the pack of cards and, as you do so, glance at the bottom card of the cut. If the card is a different value or colour to the chosen card, the chosen card is an 'after' card. If it is the same colour and value as the face-up card, the chosen card is a 'before' card. It is important to remember this for the trick to work.

3 Complete the cut by putting the bottom pile on top of the face-up card and square up the pack.

4 Repeat this process another once or twice, depending on how confident you are with your memory skills! So again, fan through the pack and ask the spectator to choose a card. Cut the deck at that point, putting the cut cards under the pack. Tell the spectator to turn over her card then cut the pack again, glimpsing the bottom card of the cut and noting whether this makes the chosen card a 'before' or 'after' card. Finish the cut and square up the pack.

5 It is now time to complete the trick. Fan through the pack and ask the spectator to remove her two chosen cards (they will be face up in the pack) and the card that comes immediately before or after each one. (This is where the 'before' and 'after' comes into play.)

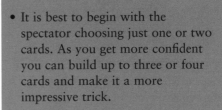

Top tips

- It is best to begin with the spectator choosing just one or two cards. As you get more confident you can build up to three or four cards and make it a more impressive trick.

- If you forget whether the card is 'before' or 'after', go with 'after' as probability states that it is extremely unlikely that the spectator will have chosen a card of the same colour and value – although you could be unlucky!

6 You should now have four playing cards on the table in front of you – two face up and two face down. Ask the spectator to turn over the face-down cards and they will be the same value and colour as the two chosen cards next to them (below).

Order in the house

The magician asks a spectator to cut the pack and remember the card that happens to be at the top of the cut section. The magician is able to tell exactly what the card is without looking at it.

Skill level ♦♦♦

Preparation

This involves quite a complicated ordering of the deck before you can begin the actual trick. First, divide the pack of cards into the four suits and put them face up in piles on the table – Spades, Hearts, Clubs then Diamonds. Next, you need to arrange the cards in columns following a specific running order, as follows:

- Spades: King, Ace, Two, and so on.

- Hearts: Ten, Jack, Queen, and so on.

- Clubs: Seven, Eight, Nine, and so on.

- Diamonds: Four, Five, Six, and so on.

You now need to assemble the deck by working across the 13 rows of four cards (right). Starting in the left-hand column, turn the King of Spades face down. Place the Ten of Hearts face down on top, followed by the Seven of Clubs and the Four of Diamonds. Do the same with the next column, starting with the Ace of Spades, face down on top of the Four of Diamonds, and so on, until the deck is complete.

How to do it

1 Ask a volunteer to cut the deck into two piles. Tell him to look at the top card from the cut section then return it. Put that pile on top of the other pile, so that his chosen card is now on top of the pack. As you square up the pack, glance at the bottom card. By adding three to its value, you can tell the value of the spectator's card. So, for example, if the bottom card is a Ten, the spectator's card is a King.

2 In order to work out the suit of the card, you need to think of the word CHaSeD. This is the order of the suits: Clubs, Hearts, Spades, Diamonds. The suit of the spectator's card will always be the one that follows that of the bottom card. So, if the bottom card is a Heart, his will be a Spade.

3 You can now reveal what the chosen card was. Ask the spectator to turn over the card, which will still be on the top of the pack, and your guess will be correct.

Top tip

To add a twist to things, both you and the spectator could write your predictions down on pieces of paper. Swap the pieces of paper, open them and lay them out on the table to show that they match.

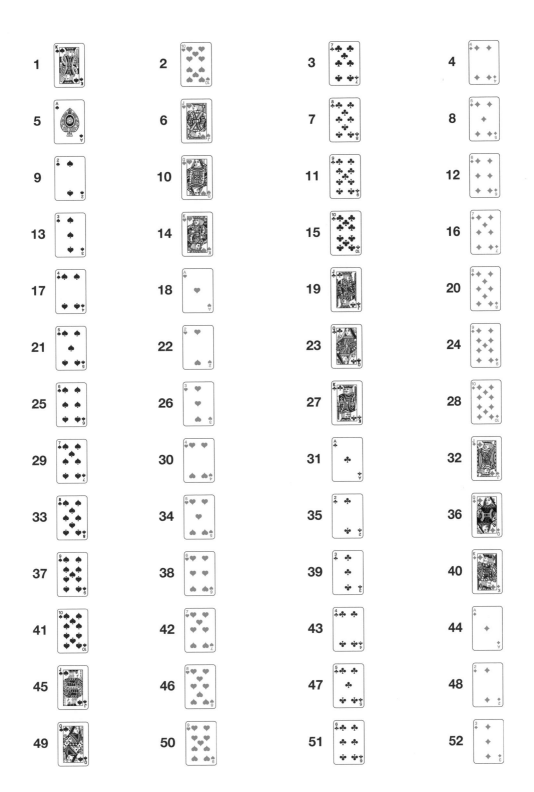

Pocket the difference

The magician deals four cards on to the table and asks a spectator to choose one of them to memorize. The magician then places all four cards in his pocket and is able to pull out the card that the spectator chose. This is a fantastic performance trick and one that is guaranteed to confuse your audience no end.

Skill level ♦♦

Preparation

Before you begin the trick place three cards in your pocket – it does not matter which three and you do not even need to look at them first.

How to do it

1 Ask a volunteer to shuffle the pack of cards and return it to you. Deal off the top four cards of the pack face up on to the table (below).

2 Ask the spectator to pick one of the cards. She should not touch it; she just needs to memorize it, as you must not know which card it is. Now gather up the cards and memorize the value of each and the order in which they appear. You do not need to worry about suits. Place the cards in your pocket, behind the three that are already there.

3 Tell the spectator to concentrate hard on her chosen card as you try to use your psychic powers to work out which one it is.

4 Remove one of the three original cards from your pocket, look at it thoughtfully for a few seconds and place it somewhere in the middle of the pack. At this stage and for the next couple of cards, you can build up the tension by reminding the spectator to concentrate really hard on her card, or that you think you have almost got it.

5 Reach back into your pocket and take the next card of the original three and once again look at it before placing it in the middle of the pack. Remember not to let the audience see these cards as they might realize that they are different from the four that were dealt on to the table. Repeat this once more with the last original card.

Top tip

To distract the audience while you are putting the three dummy cards back into the pack, try saying something like, 'No, it's definitely not that one'. You do not want anyone to ask to see the card or work out that they are different to the ones dealt out at the beginning of the trick.

6 Now ask the spectator to tell you what her chosen card was. Once she has told you, reach back into your pocket and take the relevant card from the four still there, making sure you know the position of the correct card. Bring it out of your pocket and place it face up on the table.

Quick-witted Kings

The magician shows the two black Kings to the audience and deals them face down on to the table. A spectator picks a card from the pack and inserts it face up between the two Kings. The magician returns the cards, cuts the pack and the spectator's card moves from between the two black Kings to between the two red Kings. This quick and impressive trick requires minimal preparation and a few basic skills, such as the double lift (see page 13).

Skill level ◆◆◆

Preparation

Before you begin the trick remove all four Kings from the pack of cards. Place a red King face up on the bottom of the face-down pack and the other three Kings face down on top of the pack, with the red King between the two black Kings (below).

How to do it

1 Ask for a volunteer from the audience. Remove the top card from the pack (a black King) and show this to the audience before returning it to the pack. Now deal the card face down on to the table.

2 Perform a double lift so that the audience sees the second black King and return the cards to the pack. Now slide off just the top card and place it next to the other King, leaving a space between the cards. The audience will think this is the second black King but it is actually a red King.

3 Fan out the pack of cards, making sure that you keep the bottom card concealed, and ask the spectator to choose any card. Now ask him to place his card face up between the two face-down cards on the table.

4 Hold the main pack in your left hand and carefully ease up the top card with your little finger. Gather up the three cards – the red King, the face-up card and the black King, and place them on top of the pack.

5 Pretend to square up the pack as you lift the original top card into the other three cards and separate them from the pack. The audience will assume that you have just the three cards from the table. Flip them over and place them back on top of the pack.

6 Now slide off the two top cards and reveal that these are the two black Kings but that the spectator's card has magically disappeared from between them. Place these cards on the table.

Top tip

It is important that your audience does not see the face-up red King under the top cards, or the one at the bottom of the pack. Keep the rest of the pack squared up when you are showing the two black Kings to them, otherwise the trick will be ruined.

7 Next, cut the pack and finish the cut by placing the top section under the other pile of cards. If you are confident you can ask the spectator to cut but there is a risk that he might let the top card slide and see the face-up red King hiding underneath.

8 Now fan the pack out in front of the audience until the two red Kings are showing. Ask the spectator to remove the card that is lying between them and flip it over – it will be his card!

Perfect partners

The magician puts two random cards face up on the table and a spectator starts to deal out the remaining cards. She can choose to stop whenever she likes, at which point one of the random cards is placed on the pile and the rest of the pack is placed on top. This is repeated and the magician fans through the pack to locate the two face-up cards. The cards next to them are their partners. With a little practice this is a great trick that will impress any audience.

Skill level ♦♦♦

Preparation

Before you begin, pick out any two cards from the pack as well as their partner cards. Spades and Clubs are partners, as are Diamonds and Hearts so, for example, you could pick out the Four of Diamonds and Four of Hearts and the Ten of Clubs and Ten of Spades (below). The values of the cards are not important. Place one of each pair at the top and bottom of the pack and put the other two together somewhere in the pack, remembering roughly where you put them. It is also crucial that you remember which card is on the top and which is on the bottom of the pack.

How to do it

1 Fan through the cards, locating the partner cards hidden in the pack. Remove them, pretending that you are picking out any two random cards. Place them face up on the table.

2 Now perform a false shuffle with the remainder of the pack, keeping the top and bottom cards in place (see pages 9–10) – this is very important!

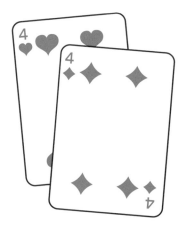

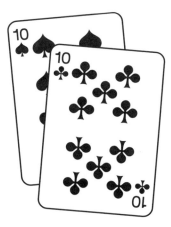

3 Hand the pack to the spectator and tell her to start dealing the cards face down on to the table, stopping whenever she likes. When she stops, place the partner card of whichever card was on the bottom of the pack face up on top of the last dealt card. There should now be one face-up card on the face-down pile of dealt cards. Ask the spectator to place the undealt pile of cards face down on top of this face-up pile (right).

4 Now ask the spectator to start dealing again, stopping whenever she wishes. When she stops, place the other face-up card on top of the dealt pile and ask her to put the remaining cards back on top.

5 Take the pack of cards back from the spectator and fan through it until you reach one of the face-up cards. Remove this card and the card to the right of it and do the same with the other face-up card. You will now have two pairs of cards on the table. Turn over the face-down cards to reveal that they are the partners of the face-up cards next to them.

Flipping amazing

The top four cards are removed from a shuffled pack and a spectator is asked to choose one of them, memorize it and replace it. The magician is able to then fan through the deck and pick out the spectator's card. This clever trick works on the principle that some cards can be identified as being upside down from the position of the symbols.

Skill level ♦♦

Preparation

Before you begin, remove the Three of Spades, Five of Hearts, Seven of Clubs and Nine of Diamonds from the pack. Line them up in that order and, looking at the central point on each card – that is, the central Spade, Heart, and so on – make sure that the Three, Five and Seven are the correct way up (the Nine will be correct whichever way it's facing.) Place the cards face down on top of the pack.

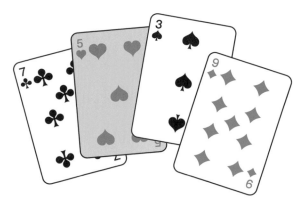

How to do it

1 Shuffle the pack in front of your audience, being careful not to disturb the top four cards (see page 12) then ask for a volunteer. Deal the top four cards face down on to the table in front of you so that they remain the correct way up.

2 Ask the spectator to choose one of the cards and memorize it. While he is doing this, gather up the remaining cards, turning them upside down as you do. Tell the spectator to put his card back anywhere among the four. He can now cut the rest of the pack wherever he likes and you insert the four cards.

3 Now fan through the deck and find the four cards. You are looking for the one among them that is now upside down – this will be the spectator's card (left). If all four are facing the same way the spectator's card is the Nine.

Tricks with props

The most spectacular magic shows are those that involve tricks with props. The greater the number of elements involved, the higher the chances of something going wrong, so pulling off an act that relies on props as well as the magician's personal skill is always going to impress. You do not have to go to great expense to perform these tricks – props are basic and include coins, matchboxes, a handkerchief and a wine glass – but you do have to practise the majority of them to carry them out with flair.

Bag of tricks

A spectator places a Joker face up into a fan of 20 face-down cards. He then memorizes the two cards either side of the Joker. The magician deals out the cards, squares them up again and places them in a bag. He then pulls the two cards that the spectator memorized out of the bag. This is one of those clever tricks that relies on showmanship as well as skill.

Skill level ♦♦

You will need
A Joker. A bag big enough to fit both hands in.

Preparation
Before you begin, place a Joker, face up, on the table. Shuffle the pack well and deal off the first 20 cards, face down, on to the table. Ask for a volunteer then square up the pile of cards and fan them out.

How to do it
1 Ask the spectator to insert the Joker face up anywhere into the face-down fan of cards. Now square up the cards and hand them to the spectator. Ask him to fan the cards out towards himself (so that the cards are all face up apart from the Joker, which is face down). Ask him to memorize the cards either side of the Joker before squaring up the pack and passing it back to you.

2 With the pile face down, deal the first card into the centre of the table. Now, starting to the right of that card and alternating between right and left, deal out all the remaining cards, making sure that you deal the last two cards on top of the right pile. Ignore the card in the centre and place the right pile on top of the left pile.

3 Repeat this process: deal the first card into the centre of the table then alternate the rest of the cards between the right and left, starting to the right. However, this time you should only deal the last card on top of the left pile instead of dealing the last two cards on top of the right pile. Place the right pile on top of the left pile.

4 Discard the cards in the centre and fan out the pile until you reach the Joker. You can also discard the Joker and move the cards above it to the bottom of the pile.

5 Now take the bag and place both hands inside it, holding the cards. Split the pile in half so you have nine cards in each hand. Turn the cards in your left hand over so that they are face up and count five cards from the top of this pile. Then count five cards from the top of the pile that is face down in your right hand. The fifth card from each pile will be the two cards that the spectator memorized.

6 Once you have located these cards, you can remove them from the bag and show them to your audience.

An open and shut case

The magician deals cards from the pack on to the table until a spectator indicates for him to stop. The spectator then opens the card box and removes a piece of paper with a card prediction written on it. On turning over the card that the magician stopped at, it is revealed that the prediction matches.

Skill level ◆◆

You will need
Pen. Paper. Card box.

Preparation
Before you begin the trick, pick any card from the pack and write its name on a piece of paper. Put this inside the empty card box. Place the card face down underneath the case and leave the case to one side on the table.

How to do it
1 Ask a volunteer to shuffle the pack as much as he likes before handing it back to you. Now begin slowly dealing cards face down into a pile on the table and tell the spectator to tell you to stop whenever he likes.

2 When you are asked to stop, set aside the remaining cards. You need to pick up the card box and the card underneath and place these on top of the dealt pile. Do this by moving your thumb slightly under one side of the card and your little finger around the other side (right).

3 As you are doing this, distract the audience by explaining that there is a prediction inside the case and you are making sure that the case connects with the cards to get the prediction correct.

4 Hand the case to the spectator and ask him to remove the piece of paper and read out the prediction. Now ask him to turn over the top card on the pile – they will be the same.

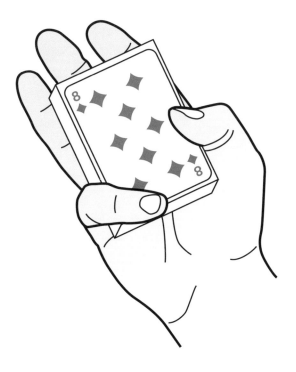

Penny pinching

The magician shuffles the pack well and fans the cards out on the table, face down. He asks a member of the audience to choose any card. The magician then takes his wallet out of his pocket and removes a card from it – the card chosen by the spectator!

Skill level ♦♦

You will need
An identical card from another pack. Double-sided sticky tape. A wallet or a purse.

Preparation
Before you begin, choose the card you want to use and take a matching one from another pack so that you have two identical cards. Place one of them inside your wallet. Now place a small strip of double-sided sticky tape on the outside of your wallet and put it back in your pocket. Place the other card face down on top of the pack of cards (below).

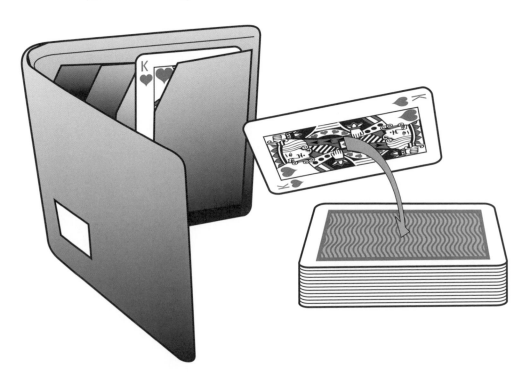

How to do it

1 Perform a false shuffle in front of your audience, ensuring that you do not disturb the top card (see page 9).

2 Fan the pack out and ask a member of the audience to pick a card, but not to look at it. Square up the pack and place the chosen card on the top.

3 Take out your wallet, place it on top of the pack with the double-sided sticky tape facing down and explain to your audience that your wallet is going to predict the chosen card. The top card will stick to the wallet. Move your wallet to the table and turn over the new top card. This is the card the spectator believes she chose but is actually the planted card.

4 Now open your wallet and take out the matching predicted card. The audience will be astounded.

Top tips

• Be really careful when placing your wallet on top of the deck – you do not want your audience to spot the tape or the card when it sticks to the bottom.

• Use a wallet or purse that is a lot bigger than the playing card to make this easier.

Raise your glass

The magician places the pack of cards in a large wine glass and announces that he is going to use a specially trained 'sniffer' card to find all the Kings in the pack. Sure enough, the sniffer card manages to locate all the Kings, without the magician touching the cards. This trick requires a bit of preparation and a certain amount of skill to pull it off. If you are performing a routine then it is a great act to finish on.

Skill level ♦♦♦♦♦

You will need
An identical pack of cards. Glue. A large wine glass. A small tea towel.

Preparation
Before you begin the trick, remove all the Kings from the pack and remove an extra Four of Hearts and Eight of Spades from another, identical, pack. Glue the two black Kings together back to back and do the same with the red Kings. Finally do the same thing with one set (one black and one red) of the identical cards. Assemble the pack of cards as follows: place the main pack face down on the table and put the Eight of Spades face up on top, followed by the double black King. Next place the double Four and Eight on top, with the Four of Hearts face up, followed by the double red King. Finish with the red Four of Hearts, face down on top. Make sure that you are sitting at one side of the table and your audience is at the other, as you need to view the opposite sides of the pack.

How to do it

1 Place the pack of cards in the wine glass so that the face-down Four of Hearts is facing you and the bottom card in the pack is facing the audience. Tell the audience you are going to use a 'sniffer' card to locate the four Kings. Slide off the face-down Four of Hearts from your side of the pack and place it face up on the other side so that the audience can see it. Your top card will now be a red King.

2 Hold the stem of the wine glass with your left hand and, with your right hand, throw the tea towel over the glass so that it covers the whole glass. Use the stem to twist the glass around so that the Four of Hearts is now facing you and the red King is facing the audience.

3 Remove the tea towel and show this first King to the audience. Now, slide the double King up from the audience's side of the pack and pass it over to your side, so that the second red King is now facing you. The audience will be looking at the identical Four of Hearts.

4 Put the tea towel back over the wine glass and turn it again. Now the audience will see their second red King and the identical Four of Hearts will be facing you.

5 Tell the audience that the 'sniffer' card has worked but you have to use a black card to find the black Kings. Slide the black and red identical pair up and over the top of the pack so that the audience is now seeing the Eight of Spades and one of the black Kings on the double card is facing you.

6 Repeat the process with the tea towel, covering the glass and turning it so that the black King now faces the audience. Once again, slide this card up and over the pack to your side so that the other King is now facing out towards you. Replace the tea towel, twist the glass and the final black King will be facing the audience.

7 Complete the trick by placing the tea towel back over the wine glass in a final flourish.

Top tip

Experiment with several sizes of wine glass to find one that is large enough to accommodate a pack of cards but not so large that the pack flops about, revealing the double-sided cards.

The disappearing coin

A coin is placed in the centre of the table, a card is placed on top of the coin and a matchbox is placed on top of the card. The magician claps his hands, lifts the card and the coin has disappeared. The magician then opens the matchbox and the coin drops to the table. This is an easy trick that is perfect for children's parties.

Skill level ♦♦

You will need
A matchbox. A small magnet. Two magnetic coins.

Preparation
Before you begin the trick, place the magnet and one of the coins inside the matchbox. Position them carefully so that the magnet is at the back of the matchbox and the coin is towards the front (below). The two objects should not be touching.

Top tips

- It is important that the audience does not see the magnet inside the matchbox, so you might want to secure it towards the back end with a little sticky tape.

- Not all coins are magnetic, so check before you begin or the trick will not work!

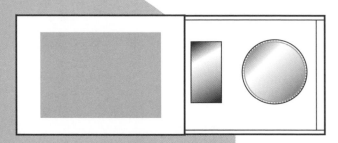

How to do it
1 Place the second coin in the middle of the table. Tell your audience that you are going to make sure the coin does not move anywhere by placing a card over it and a matchbox over the card. Do this, making sure that the matchbox is placed in such a way that the magnet is over the coin on the table.

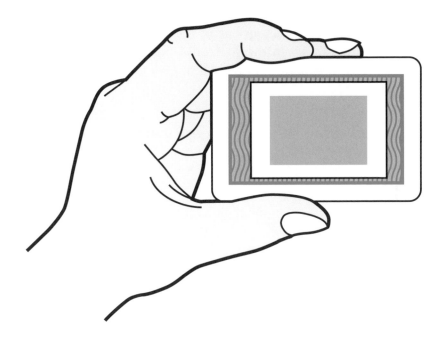

2 Clap your hands three times then lift up the card (with the matchbox on top of it) with your left hand to reveal that the coin has vanished (above).

3 Look a little confused and search the table as if you were not expecting the coin to vanish. Move your fingers underneath the card so that they support the coin and will prevent it falling when the magnet moves. Your thumb should be over the matchbox.

4 Shake the matchbox a little, bringing it up towards your ear but being careful not to reveal the coin under the card. Carefully slide the matchbox open a little way and remove the other coin, announcing to the audience that you thought it could not have got far.

The disappearing card

The magician spreads out a pack of cards roughly on the table and announces that he is going to make one of them disappear. Using a handkerchief the magician picks up one of the cards. With a wave of his hand the card disappears magically from beneath the handkerchief. On this occasion, it is the card that disappears – a great illusion that will keep your audience guessing.

You will need
A toothpick. Scissors. Handkerchief (dark colour with a hem).

Skill level ♦♦♦

Preparation
Before you begin the trick you need to cut a toothpick to match the shorter length of a playing card. Insert it into the hem of the handkerchief, so that it is positioned roughly at the centre of the edge of the handkerchief (below).

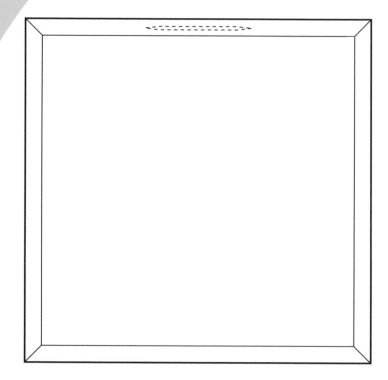

How to do it

1 Take the pack of cards and spread them out randomly on the table in front of the audience. Tell the audience that you are going to pick up a card with the handkerchief and make it disappear.

2 Keep the edge of the handkerchief with the toothpick hidden as you drop it on top of the pile of cards. Put your hand over it and feel until you have located the toothpick.

3 Now you need to hold the toothpick between your finger and thumb and carefully lift the handkerchief up by the toothpick, so that it looks as if you are lifting up one of the cards behind the raised handkerchief (above).

4 Gently wave the handkerchief around over the other cards, being careful not to let it sway too much as this will reveal that there is nothing really underneath.

5 Now start to wave it a little more quickly then grab the handkerchief with your other hand, releasing the toothpick, and show that the card has now disappeared.

Torn apart

A spectator picks a card from the pack. The magician then tears the card into six, secures the pieces together with a paper clip and holds them in one hand. The magician then blows on his hand, opens it and, sure enough, the pieces of card have blown away, leaving just the paper clip. The magician then asks the spectator to turn over the top card on the pack and it is his!

Skill level ♦♦♦♦♦

You will need

A large paper clip. A pocket fan.

Preparation

Before you begin the trick, place the paper clip and pocket fan in your right pocket. You need to make sure that the paper clip is not too tight; loosen it a little so it is easy to slide off the cards but not obvious to the audience.

How to do it

1 Shuffle the pack in front of your audience and fan the cards out face down on the table.

2 Ask for a volunteer to point to any card but not to look at it. Cut the pack to bring the chosen card to the top, then square up the pack and hold it in your left hand.

3 Perform a double lift (see page 13) with your right hand. The spectator will, seeing the second card in the pack, assume that it is his. Ask him to memorize the card then turn the two cards face down again and place them back on the pack.

4 Now slide off the real top card and put the rest of the pack to one side. Tear the card into six pieces, being careful not to let the face of the card show, and put them in your left hand.

5 Use your right hand to take the paper clip out of your pocket and secure the pieces of card together in your right hand.

6 You now need to pretend that you are passing the pieces back to your left hand and using your right hand to go back into your pocket. What you actually need to do is pass the paper clip into your left hand and keep the pieces of card in your right hand. When you go into your pocket to get the fan, you leave the pieces of card in there.

7 Take the fan out of your pocket and tell your audience that you are going to try and blow the pieces of card out of your hand. Switch on the fan and hold it above your left hand for a few seconds.

8 Now open your hand to reveal the paper clip but no pieces of card (left). Move the pack back into the centre of the table and ask the spectator to turn over the top card. He will be amazed to see that it is the card he chose at the beginning of the trick.

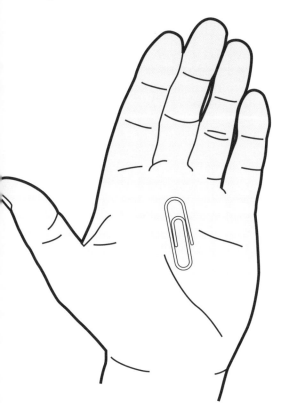

The veil of mystery

The magician places the pack of cards under a napkin and asks a member of the audience to cut the pack. He is then able to guess which card is now on the top of the pack.

Skill level ♦

You will need
A large napkin.

Preparation
Before facing your audience and starting the trick, memorize the card on top of the pack.

Top tip

This is a great dinner party trick as you can use a napkin from the dinner table and will have a captive audience.

How to do it

1 Shuffle the pack in front of your audience, making sure you do not disturb the top card (see page 9).

2 Holding the pack of cards in one hand, place the napkin over the top with the other. As you do this, turn the pack over in your hand so that it is face up and the memorized card is now at the bottom of the pile.

3 Ask a member of the audience to put her hand under the napkin and cut the pack, while you are still holding it face up. Discretely twist the half pack remaining in your hand back over again, so it is face down. Still under the napkin, take the cut half from the volunteer and place it underneath the cards in your hand. Flick the napkin away. Predict the top card and ask the spectator to remove it and show it to the rest of the audience.

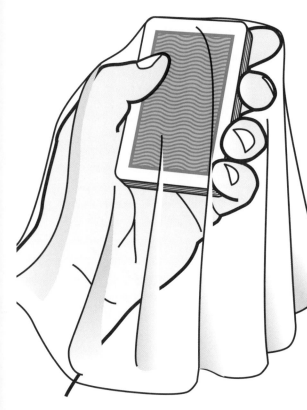

Balancing act

The magician places a card on his finger and puts a coin on top of it. He asks a spectator to do the same and then issues a challenge to the spectator to remove the card without disturbing the coin. The spectator tries and fails but the magician performs the challenge seamlessly. This trick requires a good deal of practise and is all about positioning the card and coin in exactly the right spot and being able to balance them at the end of your finger.

Skill level ♦♦♦♦

You will need
Two small coins.

How to do it

1 Place any card at the end of your left index finger. Now place the coin exactly over the tip of your finger. It is crucial to get this right or the coin will not stay balanced.

2 Ask for a volunteer from the audience and tell her to copy what you have done – placing a card on her index finger and a coin on top.

3 Now challenge her to remove the card without touching the coin or disturbing it in any way.

4 She will inevitably fail to do this and you can then complete the challenge by doing it yourself as follows.

5 When you are happy that the card and coin are in the correct position, use the index finger of your right hand to flick the card quite firmly along one short edge. You should flick up against the edge of the card and the card will fly away, leaving the coin on your finger.

Index

Acknowledgements

Executive Editor: Trevor Davies

Editor: Leanne Bryan

Executive Art Editor: Karen Sawyer

Designer: Martin Lovelock

Illustrations: Brindeau Mexter, Line + Line and Publish on Demand Ltd

Senior Production Controller: Martin Croshaw